COLLECTED POEMS

Eiléan Ní Chuilleanáin

COLLECTED POEMS
Eiléan Ní Chuilleanáin

Wake Forest University Press

First North American edition

First published in Ireland by
The Gallery Press and edited by Peter Fallon.

For permission, write to
Wake Forest University Press
Post Office Box 7333
Winston-Salem, NC 27109
WFUPRESS.WFU.EDU
WFUPRESS@WFU.EDU

ISBN 978-1-930630-96-3 (paperback)
ISBN 978-1-930630-97-0 (cloth)
LCCN 2020943388

Designed and typeset by
Nathan Moehlmann, Goosepen Studio & Press.

Publication of this book was generously
supported by the Boyle Family Fund.

for Niall, Xenya, Phoenix, and Arthur

CONTENTS

from *Acts and Monuments* (1972)

from *Site of Ambush* (1975)

from *The Rose Geranium and Other Poems* (1981)

The Magdalene Sermon (1989)

The Brazen Serpent (1994)

The Girl Who Married the Reindeer (2001)

The Sun-fish (2009)

The Boys of Bluehill (2015)

The Mother House (2019)

New Poems (2020)

Coda

COLLECTED POEMS

Eiléan Ní Chuilleanáin

from
Acts and Monuments

Lucina Schynning in Silence of the Nicht

Moon shining in silence of the night
the heaven being all full of stars
I was reading my book in a ruin
by a sour candle, without roast meat or music
strong drink or a shield from the air
blowing in the crazed window, and I felt
moonlight on my head, clear after three days' rain.

I washed in cold water; it was orange, channeled down bogs
dipped between cresses.
The bats flew through my room where I slept safely.
Sheep stared at me when I woke.

Behind me the waves of darkness lay, the plague
of mice, plague of beetles
crawling out of the spines of books,
plague shadowing pale faces with clay
the disease of the moon gone astray.

In the desert I relaxed, amazed
as the mosaic beasts on the chapel floor
when Cromwell had departed, and they saw
the sky growing through the hole in the roof.

Sheepdogs embraced me; the grasshopper
returned with lark and bee.
I looked down between hedges of high thorn and saw
the hare, absorbed, sitting still
in the middle of the track; I heard
again the chirp of the stream running.

Ransom

The payment always has to be in kind;
easy to forget, traveling in safety,
until the demand comes in.

Do not think him unkind, but begin
to search for the stuff he will accept.
It is not made easy:
a salmon, a marten-skin, a cow's horn,
a live cricket. Ants have helped me
to sort the millet and barley grains.
I have washed bloodstains from the enchanted shirt.

I left home early
walking up the stony bed
of a shallow river, meaning to collect
the breast-feathers of thousands of little birds
to thatch a house and barn.
It was a fine morning, the fields
spreading out on each side
at the beginning of a story,
steam rising off the river.
I was unarmed, the only bird
a lark singing out of reach:
I looked forward to my journey.

Wash

Wash man out of the earth; shear off
the human shell.
Twenty feet down there's close cold earth
so clean.

Wash the man out of the woman:
the strange sweat from her skin, the ashes from her hair.
Stretch her to dry in the sun,
the blue marks on her breast will fade.

Woman and world not yet
clean as the cat
leaping to the window sill with a fish in her teeth;
her flat curious eyes reflect the squalid room,
she begins to wash the water from the fish.

Swineherd

When all this is over, said the swineherd,
I mean to retire, where
nobody will have heard about my special skills
and conversation is mainly about the weather.

I intend to learn how to make coffee, at least as well
as the Portugese lay-sister in the kitchen
and polish the brass fenders every day.
I want to lie awake at night
listening to cream crawling to the top of the jug
and the water lying soft in the cistern.

I want to see an orchard where the trees grow in straight lines
and the yellow fox finds shelter between the navy-blue trunks,
where it gets dark early in summer
and the apple blossom is allowed to wither on the bough.

Waterfall

This airy afternoon, warm and free,
my head lies against the bridge,
the vibrant coping stones
arching the green insistent waterfall;
my cheek feels the cold
bricks of the cistern where Vercingetorix
died in Rome, the dark earth of London
where blood fell from O'Rourke betrayed
1591,
the cool grass of White Island
monastic, long ruined and freshly springing
in between broken walls,
carved and scattered stones.

Carrigadrohid

Celibates

When the farmers burned the furze away
where they had heedlessly lived till then
the hermits all made for the seashore,
chose each a far safe hole beneath rocks,
now more alone than even before.

Nights darker than thickest hawthorn-shade;
the march wind blew in cold off the sea.
They never again saw a sunrise
but watched the long sands glitter westwards.
Their bells cracked, their singing grew harsher.

In August a bee, strayed overboard
down the high cliff, hummed along the strand.
Three hermits saw him on that long coast.
One Spring the high tides stifled them all.

Go On Sailing

i.m. Paddy MacNeice

Now you will never see
the holly trees cut down
the houses falling
the arrival of the stellar birds
or your children's children.

Dear astronaut,
continue to explore
the chambers of the earth
winding between the submerged shells;
dear Argonaut,
go on sailing
to the center of the planet.

Letter to Pearse Hutchinson

I saw the islands in a ring all round me
and the twilight sea traveling past
uneasy still. Lightning over Mount Gabriel:
at such a distance no sound of thunder.
The mackerel just taken
battered the floor, and at my elbow
the waves disputed with the engine.
Equally grey, the headlands
crept round the rim of the sea.

Going anywhere fast is a trap:
this water music ransacked my mind
and started it growing again in a new perspective
and like the sea that burrows and soaks
in the swamps and crevices beneath
made a circle out of good and ill.

So I accepted all the sufferings of the poor,
the old maid and the old whore
and the bull trying to remember
what it was made him courageous
as life goes to ground in one of its caves,
and I accepted the way love
poured down a cul-de-sac
is never seen again.

There was plenty of time while the sea water
nosed across the ruinous ocean floor
inquiring for the ruinous door of the womb
and found the soul of Vercingetorix
cramped in a jam jar
who was starved to death in a dry cistern
in Rome, in 46 BC.

Do not expect to feel so free on land.

I Saw the Islands in a Ring All Round Me

Far from the land, they had started to grow,
far from complete, around the line of sky.
The boat edged across the circular bay
as loud as a circular saw
slicing a wake through metal.
The sea exhaled into silence, the islands
shuffled and swam. The circle
edged slowly to the west.

The pilot is the pivot
in the middle of a clockface.
The boat slides easily as the hand of a clock
measuring time at the edge of the water.
She will recall how his face
against the primrose light, the curve of his brow
interrupting the sky, cut off
an hour, the first horizon.

More Islands

A child afraid of islands, their dry
moonlit shoulders, sees in a deep gutter
a stone, a knot in the stream.
She feels the gasping of wrecks,
cormorants and lighthouses.

She grows up to detest airports
but feels the sea in the waves of her hair
and icebergs in a storm of lemonade.

She knows there are some islands the sea avoids.
Boats leaving the coastline are led far astray
by strong currents, long mackerel shoals.
High on their dark rocks a man
shouting for help, a bell ringing
can call over hundreds of high tides
and not be heard, raising no echo
until an injured seagull blown flat along the stones
touches the hard earth, or the first fire
lit by a castaway cuts the darkness
liberating silence.

Ferryboat

Once at sea, everything is changed:
even on the ferry, where
there's hardly time to check all the passports
between the dark shore and the light,
you can buy tax-free whiskey and cigars
(being officially nowhere)
and in theory get married
without a priest, three miles from the land.

In theory you may also drown
though any other kind of death is more likely.
Taking part in a national disaster
you'd earn extra sympathy for your relations.

To recall this possibility the tables and chairs
are chained down for fear of levitation
and a death's-head in a lifejacket grins beside the bar
teaching the adjustment of the slender tapes
that bind the buoyant soul to the sinking body,
in case you should find yourself gasping
in a flooded corridor or lost between cold waves.

Alive on sufferance, mortal before all,
shipbuilders all believe in fate.

Survivors

Where the loose wheel swings at the stern
of Noah's ark, I can see the man himself
deathmask profile against a late sunrise
bleeding profusely from a wound in his throat.

On deck the mouse wakes up, stretches,
edges to shelter to watch the cat.
The other mouse has stopped trying to distract him.
She does not know the beasts of prey
have all been brainwashed. Their ascetic pose
should last the voyage.

No winds compel us eastward or
westward propel seeds of plants
or the smell of decomposing systems.
If the water drains we may see
again our flooded springtime, scarred
with damp, leaves clinging together
like the pages of a sunk book,
the graves of the dead washed clean.

The bloodstained shirt stiffens
turns brown at the shoulder; the blood
edges down the sleeve, soft with a fresh smell.

The animals think they are being taken somewhere.
Do they all want to survive? They allow me
to lock their kennels at sunset, feed them
turnips, even the carnivores.
Their drink is juice of the flood.

Please go easy with the blood.
It's not as if we had that much to spare;
the human ration has been cut
to a gallon a head, and the heads have been cut
as a temporary measure to me and you.

The menagerie expects a future and you
crouching on the deck against my knees
let it drip on my wet skirt
soak in with dust and rain
lodged firmly until the blood of the saints
rises vertically smelling of ink
from sawdust, flagstones, seacaves, to explain.
While the blood still seeps down
I drink it steadily myself
(I have to think of the passengers)
my teeth ploughing in your throat.

I feel now so old I can barely remember
how it was before I was conceived.
I recall a shining egg-shaped ocean
foul as a deserted egg;
it weighed down on the sea bed
like the fat arse of Leviathan
pressing the lives out of lobsters, cracking the ribs of wrecks;
nothing was able to move.
How peaceful it was, long ago!

The Second Voyage

Odysseus rested on his oar and saw
the ruffled foreheads of the waves
crocodiling and mincing past: he rammed
the oar between their jaws and looked down
in the simmering sea where scribbles of weed defined
uncertain depth, and the slim fishes progressed
in fatal formation, and thought

                          if there was a single
streak of decency in these waves now, they'd be ridged
pocked and dented with the battering they've had,
and we could name them as Adam named the beasts,
saluting a new one with dismay, or a notorious one
with admiration; they'd notice us passing
and rejoice at our shipwreck, but these
have less character than sheep and need more patience.

I know what I'll do he said;
I'll park my ship in the crook of a long pier
(and I'll take you with me he said to the oar)
I'll face the rising ground and walk away
from tidal waters, up riverbeds
where herons parcel out the miles of stream,
over gaps in the hills, through warm
silent valleys, and when I meet a farmer
bold enough to look me in the eye
with "where are you off to with that long
winnowing fan over your shoulder?"
there I will stand still
and I'll plant you for a gatepost or a hitching-post
and leave you as a tidemark. I can go back
and organize my house then.

                                  But the profound
unfenced valleys of the ocean still held him;
he had only the oar to make them keep their distance;
the sea was still frying under the ship's side.
He considered the water lilies, and thought about fountains
spraying as wide as willows in empty squares,
the sugarstick of water clattering into the kettle,
the flat lakes bisecting the rushes. He remembered spiders and frogs
housekeeping at the roadside in brown trickles floored with mud,
horse troughs, the black canal, pale swans at dark:
his face grew damp with tears that tasted
like his own sweat or the insults of the sea.

Going Back to Oxford

Something to lose; it came in the equipment
alongside the suicide pill and the dark blue card:
"I am a Catholic, please send for a priest"
with a space below for the next of kin.

Something to lose; and going back to Oxford,
though not for good this time, I lose it again
as the city advances like an old relation
it's no use insulting.
Notice how she repeats her effects,
the Victorian towers after the mediaeval slum,
as a yawn turns into a shiver and the air
bites like a mold pulling me north
to the evacuated roads.
Here the eye shrinks from what it sees,
the toothmarks are showing where the sharp spires got me;
and I agree to being chewed because
all that time I was looking for a reliable experience
and here it is: I give in every time,
repeat the original despair.
This is where I learned it.

Because pleasure is astonishing, but loss
expected, never at a loss for words;
tear ducts built in at birth: something to lose:
the best kind of innocence, which is not to have been afraid,
lost according to plan; and here I am, walking
through old streets to a familiar bed.

The Retreat

The long way round proved shortest in the end.
Theseus ten years after he met the bull
still stroked the thread with blistered fingers
dying to snap it and plunge
off in the maze. Only curiosity stopped him.
He missed the safety of a fight,
the yellow flame sliding and spreading
from roof to roof.
                              Skirting the warm pit
he saw he had company. A corrupted army
fled along narrowing paths:
whenever one died the corridors rang with doubt.

The bull still squatted in the gate and smiled
and the man never raised a hand.

Unconsciously by now they breathed with gills
continuing their search in the sewers;
those who held out found out, pot-holing
in the crevices of pain,
the long way round was shorter in the end.

A Midwinter Prayer

In winter's early days, the exile takes the road—
dangerous nights with ghost abroad:
the eve of Samhain in the High King's hall
Fionn stood all night, his eyes open
for well-armed demons, for fire, music and death.

The wanderer catches light from chapel doors.

> (He recalls a little boy running
> up and down the same steps
> doing the Ins and Outs:
> a Plenary Indulgence every five minutes
> to lighten the penance of Fenian men
> awaiting liberation from demons underground.)

In silence the festival begins,
human words are all spilled and soaked into the brown earth.
The silent holiday of Munster
where the dead lie more at ease
warmer than ever under the loud northern
remembrance. The uprooted love
that fed them once collapses
into their graves like cut flowers.

The final Sunday after Pentecost the priest
announced the Last Day, when the dead will spring
like shrubs from quaking earth.
Against that spring the dark night sways
waving grey plumes of smoke over the edge of the world.

> (He sees, westward again, the islands
> floating lightly as bunches of foam
> alongside the neat schooner. There
> yellow apples constantly in season
> bend high branches, and the exile
> is comforted in an orchard.)

The road stretches like the soul's posthumous journey.
The holly trees were falling already
when he left; the delicate high houses were rotting
in rain.

(He could remember summer barricades
defended on top by a row of nettles)

and all his life seemed like a funeral journey
and all his company a troop
of anxious gravediggers.
—And is that the young son
I carried through the wet and dry months?
said the mother.

The air turned cold
icicles began to grow,
frost enameled windows
and branches bent under snow.
All that the cold touched, alive or dead,
changed. A time of plenty:
ships tied up at the quay
unloading crates of raisins, mandarins,
yellow apples for the feast.

Touched by cold, the girl gave birth in a ruin:
frost made angels echo behind the sky;
the cold stars offered gifts of incense and hard gold.
The snow spared the growing seed
as the year swung round to a new birth.

The exile is a wise man with a star and stable;
he is an unpeopled poet staring at a broken wall.
He tours the excavations of east and west,
he sleeps in a cart by a river
blocked by old barbed wire and dead dogs.

When February stirs the weeds
he'll start again moving to the west
rounding the earth to recover his lost islands.
He shelters in the ruined house
where in dead silence the plaster falls
from ceilings, hour by hour. Those islands—
under his skull, under wave, underground?

He walks the streets as the celebrations begin.
Work accelerates: turkeys are crated,
bottles shift on shelves. He is jostled by baskets.
Now trampling feet remind his ears of hammers
of a hundred smiths constructing the new model of the world
turning in time to music or the circulation of the blood
where love will not be out of season or a man out of place.
The seed laid in the dead earth of December
may yet grow to a flowering tree above ground.
He will sail in a ring of welcoming islands—
midwinter, he can only pray to live that long.

The House of Time

The bird is roasting in the oven,
in the kitchen, in the house of Time.
Fat dripping into the pan,
twenty minutes to the pound and
twenty minutes over.
No clock down here, so run up to the street.
There every day the clock beams round and fair.

Where the captive lies in the cellar
no seasons baste his skin.
He guesses at summer and winter
by the vigor of his shortlived fleas.

The eight-day clock in the bedroom
survives without water,
would like to close its eyes, compelled to keep account—
the phoenix combs his memories like sand.

In the kitchen yesterday's milk
sours quietly, a poisoned fly
falls in to an early death.

Dead Fly

Sparafucile fought his peasant war
although his grey crudely-slung chassis lacked
the jet lines of midge or mosquito,
the wasp's armor, the spider's intellectual speed;
still the rough guerilla survived my stalking,
until by mistake I closed a bible
and cramped his limbs to soak in his scarce blood.

A monk that read this book and lived alone
domesticated an insect of your kind,
taught him to stand and mark the words on the page
and live in peace inside the same stone house
with a mouse he kept to bite his ear
whenever he winked, and a cock that blasted him
out of his bed for matins in the dark.

Planting these three companions as watchmen
at the frontiers of his ambition, he forgot
mortality, till death knocked them off in a row.
He complained to his friend the exile, across the profound
indelible sea. Roused by the frosty wind
of a friend's voice, the thought of home stinging
fresh and sweet as the smell of oranges,

he considered the island, so far away now it shone
bright as a theory or a stained-glass window,
colored and clear in the sun, his austere mind
half sure he had invented it, and replied:
to possess is to be capable of loss
which no possible profit can reconcile
as David, his kingdom sure, could not forget Saul.

The House Remembered

The house persists, the permanent
scaffolding while the stones move round.
Convolvulus winds the banisters, sucks them down;
we found an icicle under the stairs
tall as a church candle;
it refused to answer questions
but proved its point by freezing hard.

The house changes, the stones
hidden under dry lichen spreading
abusing the doorposts, frost on the glass.
Nothing stays still, the house is still the same
but the breast over the sink turned into a tap
and coming through the door all fathers look the same.

The stairs and windows waver but the house stands up;
peeling away the walls another set shows through
and somebody was born in every room.

The Apparition

The circular white sun
leapt overhead and grew
red as a rose, darkening slowly blue.
And the crowd wept, shivering,
standing there in the cold.

The sharp-eyed girl miraculously
cured by a beggar passed the word along.
Water, she said, and they found a spring
where all before was dry.
They filled the jars with the water.

All will be forgiven, good and evil together.
You are all my children. Come back
in mist or snow, here it will be warm.
And forget the perishing cold,
the savage light of day.

Every Friday at noon the same;
the trains were full of people in the evenings
going north with gallons of sour water.

Antediluvian

At some time previous to the destruction of the villages,
we find references to a young man "about eight feet tall"
naked and smooth with a knife loose in his hand
for pruning the lazy branches
trailed across his path.
He showed up at one time or another
in several villages, but walked through
without stopping or staying a word.
The people reacted with admiration and surprise,
running to their doors to see, watching him out of sight.

And when the snakes were handsome in the grass
the people in the villages used to
fill tin baths with enormous bunches
of bananas, and carry them laboriously down
to the main road, and offer them to travelers.

Foreseeable Future

Not immediately, but
the day will arrive for my last communion
when I plan to swallow the universe like a raw egg.
After that there will be no more complaining.

Why did I wait so long?
you may well ask: the plan is such an old one,
even as a baby I might have been sucking away:
I might have cut my teeth on it,
nibbling off a bit every morning.
I was too modest and doubted my capacity
to consume it all singlehanded; I feared
dying and leaving behind a half-chewed world.

So I was perfecting the stretch of my jaws,
padding my teeth like the hammers of a grand piano
to save the works from shock;
like the crocodile that ate the alarm clock
I mean it to go on ticking.
This is going to be a successful swallow.
How could I have lived so long
if I had not known that day
was bound to come in the end?

Family

Water has no memory
and you drown in it like a kind of absence.
It falls apart
in a continual death
a hundred-gallon tank as
innocent as outer space.

Earth remembers
facts about your relations;
wood passes on patristic
characteristics,
bone and feather,
scandal,
charcoal remembering
and every stone recalls its quarry and the axe.

Exhumation

Several times projected, a poem
clean and convincing as a new bathroom
or the inside of somebody's mouth
to explode shadows with light, reinstate love.

But
how can love do anything
not being anything itself
but a tendency to conspire with its object
as dust settles on a statue
cumulative shell.

Or more like snow hardening
in strata, grey to blank white
producing paralysis.

Listen while your friends talk approvingly of war
and you become their shadow.
It will take some archaeology
to disinter gently
the historical ages and layers of love.

Lost Star

Starting from the window, the bars
and the three brick walls, the cherry tree
in the center of the yard, most of its leaves
lying light as feathers beneath, but some
still clinging by twos and threes—
not enough to shield the planet
hanging there like a fruit

but further away than it seems—
can I really see you swinging
around me now in a circle
whose radius is longer than the arms of any known clock?

The lonely pilot guides
the lost star, its passengers the crowd
of innocents exiled in winter.
Sometimes, letting the vessel drift
into danger, he pauses
to feed them at his miraculous breast.
Distant as the spirit imprisoned
in a bronze vase buried in shingle
at the clean edge of the sea,
floating like instantaneous foam or an island,
sealed off like a womb,

here where I sit so still
I can see the milk in my glass is tidal
inclining towards you across the dangerous sky.

Early Recollections

If I produce paralysis in verse
where anger would be more suitable
could it be because my education
left out the sight of death?
They never waked my aunt Nora in the front parlor;
our cats hunted mice but never
showed us what they killed.
I was born in the war but never noticed.
My aunt Nora is still in the best of health
and her best china has not been changed or broken.
Dust has not settled on it; I noticed it first
the same year that I saw
how the colors of stones change as water
dries off them after rain.
I know how things begin to happen
but never expect an end.

Dearest,
        if I can never write "goodbye"
on the torn final sheet, do not
investigate my adult life but try
where I started. My
childhood gave me hope
and no warnings,
I discovered the habits of moss
that secretly freezes the stone
rust softly biting the hinges
to keep the door always open.
I became aware of truth
like the tide helplessly rising and falling in one place.

Evidence

Along the wandering strand the sea unloads glass balls
jellyfish, broken shells, its tangle
of nets, cork, bits of wood,
coral. A crooked line paid out on sand.
Here's evidence; gather it all up.

Time on windowpanes
imposes a curved edge of dust,
hides dirt under the refrigerator, invites
the mice inside to dodge
behind the revealing stack of empty bottles.
In the refrigerator the ice is growing
into odd shapes; outside
the house, the cracks are spreading
in the asphalt; they reach out, join
to weave some kind of message.

Age creates
people whose wrinkles betray
how they smiled, with scars
of operations. They have white patches
where the sun has not reached them,
the skin grows hard on their hands;
some of them have false teeth.
The flick of their lashes, the flutter of their shirtfronts
is evidence of life.

Deaths and Engines

We came down above the houses
in a stiff curve, and
at the edge of Paris airport
saw an empty tunnel—
the back half of a plane, black
on the snow, nobody near it,
tubular, burnt-out and frozen.

When we faced again
the snow-white runways in the dark
no sound came over
the loudspeakers, except the sighs
of the lonely pilot.

The cold of metal wings is contagious:
soon you will need wings of your own,
cornered in the angle where
time and life like a knife and fork
cross, and the lifeline in your palm
breaks, and the curve of an aeroplane's track
meets the straight skyline.

The images of relief:
hospital pajamas, screens round a bed,
a man with a bloody face
sitting up in bed, conversing cheerfully
through cut lips:
these will fail you sometime.

You will find yourself alone
accelerating down a blind
alley, too late to stop
and know how light your death is;
you will be scattered like wreckage;
the pieces every one a different shape
will spin and lodge in the hearts
of all who love you.

Acts and Monuments

In imitation of the weed
which out of soft enclosing mud
as from a hand that holds a lead
leans after the escaping flood,

or when warm summer stunts the flow
in tangled coils lies tired and fine,
or in calm weather stands tiptoe
to peer above the waterline,

the rooted trees bend in the wind
or twist and bow on every side;
the poplar stands up straight and slim;
but their blood cannot flower or fade

like weeds that rot when rivers dry.
Their roots embrace the stony plain,
their branches move as one, they try
to freeze the effects of wind and rain,

and like the waterline the sky
lids and defines the element
where no unformed capricious cry
can sound without its monument.

Darkening All the Strand

The light neglects her face
to warm the fruited stone
walls rising against her
across brown spiral waves
of the wandering Boyne.

What retreat, convent, group
of Gaelic-speaking vets
or Home for Protestant
Incurables, behind
those pointed windows, breathes?

Somebody walked, along
the sloped geranium
path to the damp steps where
a painted gate is shut.
New ropes hold a dark boat.

(Bright streak, brown shape.) Water-
sodden, the near flat shore
accumulates floated
light weathered filterings
that shift under her feet,

the firm ground flood-riddled;
this historical shore
clings to the evening shade—
a difficult stance for
viewing the greenhouses

(though sunlit to the left
between a half-grown hedge
plainly visible is
the nuns' graveyard, the small
ranged uniform crosses.)

The cloistered Boyne gropes on
washing out of the land's
interrelated roots,
under foundations, far
streams the nuns may recall.

Monochrome

What she saw on opening
her eyes was his darkened
coastline slipping rapidly astern
in twilight, and the waves evenly sighing.

His promontory forehead looked far off—
it seemed she had never been there—
the wide eyes shuttered pale,
as cat and mouse at night are the same color.

Love like a marmalade cat
slipped out between the bars of the scullery window
leaving the tabby and the mouse in charge
alert, straining night after night
suspiciously at each other's shadows.

from

Site of Ambush

The Lady's Tower

Hollow my high tower leans
back to the cliff; my thatch
converses with spread sky,
heronries. The grey wall
slices downward and meets
a sliding flooded stream
pebble-banked, small diving
birds. Downstairs my cellars plumb.

Behind me shifting the oblique veins
of the hill; my kitchen is damp,
spiders shaded under brown vats.

I hear the stream change pace, glance from the stove
to see the punt is now floating freely
bobs square-ended, the rope dead level.

Opening the kitchen door
the quarry brambles miss my hair
sprung so high their fruit wastes.

And up the tall stairs my bed is made
even with a sycamore root
at my small square window.

All night I lie sheeted, my broom chases down treads
delighted spirals of dust: the yellow duster glides
over shelves, around knobs: bristle stroking flagstone
dancing with the spiders around the kitchen in the dark
while cats climb the tower and the river fills
a spoonful of light on the cellar walls below.

The Breeches Buoy

Scan the close grains of the hillside;
it rises above sea pinks and a dark cliff.
A foothold, and long green leaves of sorrel
crouch at heel. Ascend
in a stirrup of rock, reaching at stems of weeds.
Bite the bitter leaf.
                    Across
a sidling sheep's track and into stony ground:
heads of new fern less than knee high
tight coiled like snails: to reach deep grass
at the field's edge: trefoil and daisy.

Fresh wheat combs the slope, it rises until
now I can see the shifting floor
the Atlantic on both sides of the Head.
The wind shakes the crop
blows through the coastguard station blackened by fire.
Troops of grey birds in a ploughed field
all face out to sea, and beyond them
notched with storms, the breeches buoy.

The Absent Girl

The absent girl is
conspicuous by her silence
sitting at the courtroom window
her cheek against the glass.
They pass her without a sound
and when they look for her face
can only see the clock behind her skull;

grey hair blinds her eyes
and night presses on the windowpanes,

she can feel the glass cold
but with no time for pain
searches for a memory lost with muscle and blood—
she misses her ligaments and the marrow of her bones.

The clock chatters; with no beating heart
lung or breast how can she tell the time?
Her skin is shadowed
where once the early sunlight fell.

The Persians

The dawn breeze came transparent spiraling out of the cliff
and the Persian host
looked along the small path and saw (though not all
really died that day)
that each had come to the place of his own death.

A man to flog the sea! But this was worse. Below
already in the pass
the losers were attentive, longhaired. Too far to come,
a wave going nowhere.

Behind them only the captains waving whips.
No turning on the mountain road and hard to breathe:
by now their lives were nothing
but flowing away from them, breath blood and sweat,
feeling the need of two faces
or a wall.
            If there had been a wall
they would have climbed and then forgotten it. They had passed
all the valleys of darkness and now
could remember only the ridges of the sea
and slowly climbing waves of sleep.

The body had changed, become the center of their world
and the world changed
so the body could not live inside it, took off
deathward, a high tide
crowding round them like the towers of Babel again.
Poor straying barbarians. By now the rocks
against them were blinding;
and one Persian thought about the patch of hard earth
seen through a slit
in a jail wall, dear as a kind marked hand,

while one recalled, but could not think
where he had seen it, a moving circle—
sky over a high narrow tower .
as blank and remote as a child's eye.

April 71

The stench of summer lying cold last April
weeds had begun blocking the stream

men breathing whole, their bones
were beginning to crack

a green pocket of time, like a valley
only birds can see

this month light grows longer
still we have not watched the silent window
bleaching towards dawn

Manuscript Found in a Bottle

After a week at sea
they wake, the boards are damp
easily rocking, sloped away
from the sun. There sits our captain on the right
beginning the study of navigation
with an astrolabe.

A dark wall sways above, hiding the sunrise,
the height of noon.
Upstage, long flat shadows like a railway station
where the others crouch stranded.
Out of their stripe of darkness their quick breath
ruffles the sheer daylight, while
they hatch small bundles towards angular death
backing the cool wall, and one, a girl, watches for fish
in empty sea, crooning to the salt wave:

    water soaks in wood
    you can sleep safe as
    bats in a tunnel
    water will reach you
    you can curl up like
    cats on a mealbag
    your whiskers will soon
    begin to feel cold.

The polar stars have left our sky,
here in the lap of the wind it is cold;
not an island nor a rock to mar
the slippery face of water—
at evening a whine, high up, of branches;
flats of rain stretch out
diagonal between the grottoes and side chapels of the air,
the grey sea tilts at wind;
…and now far below, the yellow sand revolving,
our corner is thick with a drift of brown beech leaves.

Old Roads

Missing from the map, the abandoned roads
reach across the mountain, threading into
clefts and valleys, shuffle between thick
hedges of flowery thorn.
The grass flows into tracks of wheels,
mowed evenly by the careful sheep;
drenched, it guards the gaps of silence
only trampled on the pattern day.

And if, an odd time, late
at night, a cart passes
splashing in a burst stream, crunching bones,
the wavering candle hung by the shaft
slaps light against a single gable
catches a flat tombstone
shaking a nervous beam as the hare passes.

Their arthritic fingers
their stiffening grasp cannot
hold long on the hillside—
slowly the old roads lose their grip.

Aherlow

As I woke up I heard the sergeant say
can you not hear the bugle calling?
Brush your hair, put clean sheets on your bed
you lazy Hirish ound
and I woke before Sebastopol
far from home.

As we went on sailing through a dark ocean
and at long intervals a buzzer called for help—
sailing through perpendicular seas
head downward like Dracula
towards the burning mountain—
sailing down the north side of the mind,
I heard our captain saying,
"Remember both that seed and stem both yours
not for a feral life, but to pursue
knowledge and virtue's difficulty."
And islanded in pain
I woke before Sebastopol.

Dreaming in the Ksar es Souk Motel

I

The hard sand
molded like the sea
sleeps out dawn
planing east

in shallow scoops of light
folding over caves and graves

she sails within glass walls
as in a ship, her mouth
dry with air that hisses
in iron corridors
her food smells of engines
her share of water glows in a jug

a soft hum between
her and the bird's cry
outside she sees dogs
in dry riverbeds

silent faces dark as the bark of trees
pausing watch her drink

...there were roads
for wide-eyed fish muscling along
she could see palms waving mile by mile.
Here she never tasted salt, but backward
and forward in its short cage while she slept
the square swimming pool pounded.

II

Shift-click of night wave
knight's move of current
switching tides in a small square bay

to land below grey pointed houses looming
in clear air of daybreak
and a remote bell scares the flatfoot gulls
walking up the ferry road
while from a chimney crest a blackbird looks
severely down.

The bell rings seaward
then reverberates uphill
where the pale road curves away
between dry white convent walls.

Standing on the wet flagstones you can see
only the sidling road.
But follow the sound,
there are steps, lanes,
high walls, darkness of sandstone
valerian springing from cracks
gutters and the ridges water makes in earth.

Out of sight the rivers persist
they riddle the city, they curve and collect
making straight roads crooked, they flush
in ruined mills
and murdered distilleries.

III

It has to creep like water, it cannot jump or spread like fire
it needs to labor past mountains to be lost
to see the drops fall in the still.
Like snow like sleep it grows
like a dream it accumulates like a dream flows
underground and rises to be the same
it feels the drumming of the hare and it fears what's yet to come
suffering the storm and hearing the slates crash in the yard.

IV

In summer dawn a mirror shines
clear in the surprising light;
the shadows all reversed point towards the sea.

The Ropesellers

Behind the black dancers and the snakes
a soft corner of sunlight, shady counters
where new ropes are sold.
Pale, coiled tight in ranks, piled
spirals longer than a day's walk
tight as a spring.

The dancers are circling. The music goes round and round
and around the necks of their charmers the snakes
glide warmly, their heads waving, their wide-awake eyes—

I can't find fear among the beasts and strangers
but I know it in the man who sits and smokes
between two cylinders of rope.

The black dancers in the sun sweat,
the snakes follow the music, the rope
is binding them all with burdens past their strength
that weigh like childhood;
a woman ties the feet of six live hens together
a knot binding us to the first day
a child strained to move a great bundle
that lay for years in a doorway, dusty but secured
with a new yellow rope.

The ropes are searching backward even yet;
they twine with the earliest roots of trees
coiling around rocks, and the sources of streams.

Site of Ambush

You are not the sun or the moon
but the wolf that will swallow down both sun and moon.

They dance around but they must go down
you will devour them all.

The houses, flowers, the salt and ships
streams that flow down mountains, flames that burn up trees.

You are the twining gulf Charybdis
whose currents yield return to none.

II NARRATION

At alarming bell daybreak, before
scraping of cats or windows creaking over the street,
eleven miles of road between them,
the enemy commanders synchronized their heartbeats:
seven forty-five by the sun.
At ten the soldiers were climbing into lorries,
asthmatic engines drawing breath in even shifts.
The others were fretting over guns
counting up ammunition and money.
At eleven they lay in wait at the cross
with over an hour to go.
The pine trees looked up stiff;
at the angle of the road, polished stones
forming a stile, a knowing path
twisting away; the rough grass
gripped the fragments of the wall.

A small deep stream glassily descended:
ten minutes to the hour.
The clouds grew grey, the road grey as iron,
the hills dark, the trees deep,
the fields faded; like white mushrooms
sheep remote under the wind.
The stream ticked and throbbed
nearer; a boy carried a can to the well
nearer on the dark road.
The driver saw the child's back,
nearer; the birds shoaled off the branches in fright.

Deafly rusting in the stream
the lorry now is soft as a last night's dream.
The soldiers and the deaf child
landed gently in the water
they were light between long weeds
settled and lay quiet, nobody
to listen to them now.
They all looked the same face down there:
water too thick and deep to see.
They were separated for good.
It was cold, their teeth shrilling.
They slept like falling hay in waves.
Shells candied their skin; the water
lay heavy and they could not rise but coiled
by scythefuls limply in ranks.
A long winter stacks their bodies
and words above their stillness hang from hooks
in skeins, like dark nets drying,
flapping against the stream.
A watch vibrates alone in the filtering light;
flitters of hair wave at the sun.

III STANDING MAN

The last bed excavated, the long minute hand
upright on the hour,
the years in pain scored up are scattered and their tower
down: time at a stand.

And upright on horizons of storm the monumental crosses,
lone shafts like the spade
haunting the furrow's end, flourish when man's unmade
wedged in stones, sunk in mosses—

aching an upright femur can feel the tough roots close
gently over bone, stick
fast holding a smooth shaft. Only the flesh such strict
embraces knows.

IV TIME AND PLACE

The river still descends, finding
dark weedy stones of a harbor,
pale widowed houses.
Within, the slatted dark,
glint of water on a ceiling
shadow of balcony bars
above the dark knitting
across the shady presses
where the dated jam jars gloom.

The jam hardens at edges,
the grey fur fastens:
filth clinging at high tide.

Weakly the escaping tide
alone remembering alone
falling out of rockpools
waiting for the once-for-all wind.

A weakened creature in a dirty cream coat
with bare legs and a cropped head,
an empty face, staggers away from the sea
and looks up at the sun with a waiting eye,
alone remembering alone.
She fingers three coppers in her pocket;
the wind scratches her face—
dryskinned, these skeleton days
no more aware than wind of the passage of sand,
tolling of dead bells.
The wind heads for fresh water
shaking dust on her sleeve;
her parcel of bread grows moldy,
the milk in her jug sours fast under the sun.
As she turns the corner of the square
meeting a whirl of bicycle bells
the old man on the near bench
has two new grey hairs.

Before the dead underwater shining,
before the stream started
sprinkling off the mountainside
there was the scheming and steaming of the original volcanoes
and the glaciers trailing south.
There were winds combing the rocks, loaded with seeds,
repetitious layers of dust,
leaves by the harvestful piling in corners,
blankets of sun piled over
heavy with light...
forget?
            Then came the clay and the raven,
at last the spade and winding sheet.

Now all their lives on the site of the ambush
they see the dead walking ignorant and strong
as on their dying day. The grey shoulders
against a rainbow skyline approach again and stop

approach again and stop. The child's neck medal
grows glitters and breaks away spinning—
the ploughed field gleams against the sky
furrowed over and harrowed
on the ancient graves—
                              a clean sweep of clay,
leaves drifting up to the threshold of the sky…
shuffled. Start again.

V MARCH IN A GARDEN

The windows, arched, the blue granite;
branches of cherry reach
abroad like bridges, host a songbird
that was an egg last year.

Low forsythia flashes
from shade of high groined trees:
a narrow path cuts the lawn
and left to right a dark male figure
walks quickly, eyes dead ahead,
leaves a straight wake
while on high the attic windows of the city
peer like bulrushes over this broad calm pool of spring.

Elsewhere, in the garden where I saw them first
in nineteen-forty-nine, the shrubs bloom out of season,
their roots in New Zealand, their names
rusting on metal tags. The gardener
is Michael Barry, who threw the bowl
and hit the Chetwynd Viaduct. He shakes hands
and asks am I married yet.

VI VOYAGERS

Turn west now, turn away to sleep
and you are simultaneous with
Maelduin setting sail again
from the island of the white cat
to the high penitential rock
of a spiked Donegal hermit—
with Odysseus crouching again
inside a fish-smelling sealskin
or Anticlus suffocating
back in the wooden horse's womb
as he hears his wife's voice calling.

Turn westward, your face grows darker
you look sad entering your dream
whose long currents yield return to none.

VII NOW

I am walking beside Sandymount strand,
not on it; the tide is nearly at the new wall.
Four children are pushing back and forth
a huge reel that has held electric cable
they are knee deep in the water
I come closer and see they have rubber boots on.
The sand looks level but the water lies here and there
searching out valleys an inch deep. They interlock
reflecting a bright morning sky.
A man with a hat says to me "Is it coming in or going out?"
He is not trying to start something, the weather is too fine,
the hour early. "Coming in I think" I say—
I have been watching one patch getting smaller.

Other people are taking large dogs for walks—
have they no work to go to? The old baths
loom square like a mirage.
Light glances off water, wet sand and houses;
just now I am passing Maurice Craig's
and there he is reading a book at his window.
It is a quarter past ten—
he looks as if he's been at it for hours.

VIII   SITE OF AMBUSH

When the child comes back
soaked from her drowning
lay fast hold of her
and do not let go

your arms will be burnt
as she turns to flame
yellow on your dress
a slight flowering tree
a muscular snake
spidery crawling
becoming a bird
then an empty space

seawaves overwhelm
your arms your hair and
wind bites them until
shivering naked
the child exhausted
comes back from her sleep

          —troubling for a minute the patient republic
of the spider and the fly
on the edge of the aspic stream
above the frail shadows of wreckage

the white water-plant glinting upward
while the tall tree adds a rim to its age
and water focuses to a fish jumping
the rims of time breaking slowly on the pebbles like a bell
eyes slacken under the weight
as the saint's arm began to sag
his hand spread under the warm nesting wren
but did not give way.

The spider swayed on the end of his thread
a pendulum. The child came back from the well.
Symmetrical breasts of hills criss-crossed.
The trees grew over the sun.

Ardnaturais

The steel edge of water shuts
my close horizon, shears off
continents and the courses of ships.
An island in a saucer of air
floats in the tight neck
of the bay, sealing
an intimate coastline. No pounding historical waves,
no sandribbed invasions flung
at high tide on beaches
or violent ebb sucking pebbles away.

Warm death for a jellyfish, lost
ten legs in a crinoline; the furred bee
slants down from the cliff field, straying
over salted rocks. The water
searches the branching algae and my hair
spreads out like John the Baptist's in a dish.
Shouldering under, I feel fear
as I see them plain: the soft anemone,
bladdered weed, the crouching spiked urchin, rooted
in one clutch of pebbles, their long strands
shivering under the light.

Alone in the sea: a shallow breath held stiffly:
my shadow lies
dark and hard like time
across the rolling shining stones.

Atlantis

Here I float in my glass bowl,
light wavering in water:
a thread shivers binding me
to a branching of dry pine,
I kneel in my white nightdress
and the watchful fish slide past.

A cold place with the spring tide
pulling out there like horses
but safe. Don't ever mention
Atlantis underwater;
the glass barriers are much
stronger than waves or high rocks.

II

The staggering gable…
the baby dies on the doorstep
the old mother on the hearthstone,
the globed eye expels
serrated dust in tears.

The New Atlantis

The feast of St. John, Corpus Christi Sunday,
houses breathing warmly out like stacks of hay,
windows wide, the white and yellow Papal flags
now drooped: one side of the street nods at the cool
shadow opposite sloping towards the canal's
green weed that reflects nothing. Turn a corner,
nettles lap at a high hoarding, "sites for sale,"
empty window frames, corrugated iron
in the arches of doors, old green paint softly
blistering on gates. Cross a lane: a kitchen
bare, darkening with one shadow milk bottle,
then a bright basement—a bald man in his sleeves
folding linen in a yellow room

                              …whose lives
bulge against me, as soft as plums in a bag
sagging at summer. New Atlantis presses
up from under that blunt horizon, angles
at windows like ivy, forces flags apart.

Valerian

Dateflower, wild
in Dublin in July,
dry red nodding above the lanes
Raglan Heytesbury Wellington Waterloo
where the metalworkers thrive,
and there legged-up I stretched
to grasp their tough roots
dry between the light mortar.

Below me now they bow and lean
out over the deep railway line
disappearing off to Wexford in a seagull curve.
Coats off, knees wide on the smooth stone parapet
we are leaning over to catch the hard stems
when death goes shaking beneath us like a train—
dangerous timeflower.

Cypher

My black cat lies still,
washed, in the third of her lives
veteran squatter, *porte-malheur*, she survives
absorbing light on the sill.

While I wipe and scour,
polish the glasses grimly,
the yard-shadow of the high crooked chimney
slips closer by the hour.

What man forgets, at home
in the long noons of peace
his own imprisonment or the day of his release?
Could I forget this room

this view, the cleaning habit
all shared with Pussy?
*Forsan et haec olim meminisse
iuvabit.*

The Prisoner Thinks About the Stars

The outsides of stars
are crusted, their light fretted
with dead bodies of moths.

And moving the sound they make
sibilant stiff moth wings
drowns the universal tuning fork.

They sing like whales over the prisons,
they almost bump the roof.

House of the Dead

What wind agitates the dust
inside the Etruscan tombs?
They made beds for man and wife; the servants
were buried in the hallway.
They sealed the door up and left the dead alone.

The dust in your pocket lay still;
you stretched out for your glass,
blind as an old man in a dead calm.

Now your face looks innocent
as the Atlantic stirred up in storm,
rattling its plenty on the pebbles.
The wind roared through your house and swept it clean.

Sea-squirrels

Back to the high sandstone face
westward staring, shingle in heaps
against inward nooks, flaws
where long-remembering squirrels live.

Their long corridors wink at sunset—
roll your sleeves and try one:
only pebbles and weed. Next door
wrist bitten, scruff battling

look in its red eyes: you will see
peacocks mincing along a bridge
fountains like snow descending.
They do not die at the highest of tides,
they live on seaweed.

Odysseus Meets the Ghosts of the Women

There also he saw
the celebrated women
and in death they looked askance;
he stood and faced them,
shadows flocked by the dying ram
to sup the dark blood flowing at his heel—
his long sword fending them off,
their whispering cold
their transparent grey throats from the lifeblood.

He saw the daughters, wives
mothers of heroes or upstanding kings
the longhaired goldbound women who had died
of pestilence, famine, in slavery
and still queens but they did not know
his face, even Anticleia
his own mother. He asked her how she died
but she passed by his elbow, her eyes asleep.

The hunter still followed
airy victims, and labor
afflicted even here the cramped shoulders—
the habit of distress.

A hiss like thunder, all their voices
broke on him; he fled
for the long ship, the evening sea
Persephone's poplars
and her dark willow trees.

from

*The Rose Geranium
and Other Poems*

Night Journeys

There are more changes each time I return.

Two widows are living together in the attic
among the encyclopedias
and gold vestments.
                    A fishmonger
opens his shop at the angle of the stairs.

The scullery I see has been extended,
a wide cloister, thatched, with swallows
nesting over windows, now hides the garden.

I wake in Rome, and my brother, aged fifteen, meets me.
My father has sent him with a naggin of coffee and brandy,
which I drink on the platform.

And wake again in an afternoon bed
grey light sloping from window ledge
to straw-seated armchair. I get up,
walk down a silent corridor
to the kitchen. Twilight and a long scrubbed table,
the tap drips in an enamel basin
containing peeled potatoes. A door half-open and
I can hear somebody snoring.

from *Cork*

The island, with its hooked
clamps of bridges holding it down,
its internal spirals
packed, is tight as a ship
with a name in Greek or Russian on its tail;

as the river, flat and luminous
at its fullest, images the defenses:
ribbed quays and stacked roofs
plain warehouse walls as high as churches
insolent flights of steps.

Encamped within, the hurried exiles
sheltering against the tide
a life in waiting,
waking reach out for a door and find a banister,
reach for a light and find their hands in water,
their rooms all swamped by dreams.
In their angles the weeds
flourish and fall in a week,
their English falters and flies from them,
the floods invade them yearly.

In the graveyards of the city, wells

                     of arrested sound,
the tombstones are swaying like a house of cards.

The night obscures them as the evergreens obscure
tablets fixed on their boundary walls,
they are shouldered by tall square houses
chimneys nodding to each other
over the heads of gesturing
angels, all back and no sex.

A slot of air, the snug
just wide enough for the door to open
and bang the knees of everyone inside;
you face a window blank with dust
half-inch spiderwebs
rounding the squares of glass
and a view on either hand of mirrors
shining at each other in the gloom.

A woman's head, bowed,
a glint on her forehead
obliquely seen leaning on the counter
at the end of a vista of glasses
and one damp towel.

And out of sight in the cellars
spinning in the dust
the spiders are preparing for autumn.
They weave throughout the city,
selecting the light for their traps,
they swell with darkness.

Missing from the scene
the many flat surfaces,
undersides of doors, of doormats
blank backs of wardrobes
the walls of tunnels in walls
made by wires of bells, and the shadows of square spaces
left high on kitchen walls
by the removal of those bells on their boards,

the returning minotaur pacing transparent
in the transparent maze cannot
smell out his stall; the angles all move towards him,
no alcove to rest his horns.
At dawn he collapses in the garden where
the delicate wise slug is caressing
ribbed undersides of blue cabbage leaves
while on top of them rain dances.

As the fog descends,
"What will I do in winter?" he thinks
shocked by the echoing blows
of logs unloading in courtyards
close by, on every side.

V

When you pass the doorway
you are going underground: it is light and warm
and nothing is as you expected.
A table laid since breakfast-time,
cake and sherry, with whiskey for the men.

Outside the window it is Sunday
but the neighbors' washing hangs on the line
and between the stiff squares of white cloth
just visible, a glass window,
blackness beyond
half veiled by a net curtain,
a lined curtain, a lampshade
the wooden back of a looking glass, then blackness.

We could be in any city.

Those long retreating shades,
a river of roofs inclining
in the valley side. Gables and stacks
and spires, with trees tucked between them:
all graveyard shapes
viewed from his high windowpane.

A coffin-shaped looking glass replies,
soft light, polished, smooth as fur,
blue of mown grass on a lawn,
with neckties crookedly doubled over it.

Opening the door, all walls point at once to the bed
huge red silk in a quarter of the room
knots drowning in deep mahogany
and uniform blue volumes shelved at hand.

And a desk calendar, a fountain pen,
a weighty table-lighter in green marble,
a cigar box, empty but dusted,
a framed young woman in a white dress
indicate the future from the cold mantel.

The house sits silent,
the shiny linoleum
would creak if you stepped on it.
Outside it is still raining
but the birds have begun to sing.

The shopfront says HARDWARE, and above it
a long dusty lace curtain
blows out of a window.
A grey-haired woman and a small girl
are leaning out, and I look up at them
like a fish putting its head up
to get a better view of a heron
but I can't see into the room.
They lean out to listen to the soft notes
the brass band marching away from them
downhill to the quays.
In the street, the children have all gone after the band
and the women are still silent
still pausing from their counters and shopping bags.

VIII GRAVEYARD

Small permanent houses of limestone
with no insides, dwarf
obelisks, columns
signaling like chimneys
but solid, venting no smoke or sighs.

*

Limestone, white
as cloud, moon
or broad flashed
lightning: smooth
names erased.

*

On the hilltop railed and gated
the collapsing monuments
imprison finally
the Indomitable Repealer,
the butter merchant and his wives, the nettles.

X

Leaving the holy well,
society of streams, behind
to make fields rich with butter
to create the gravel bends
and bridges with bicycles leaning against them
welcoming the stalactite and the bulrush—
ended in the short deep channels
and transformed by the windy breath,
the lough where castle rock and blasted tree
are half erased by steel grey
chiaroscuro tempest:

a circumnavigation that was
interrupted by the city. So far
the aquatic allegory.

To pursue
the desalting, the return
ironies of cloud, storm-light
demands not only
another lifetime but what can't be had:
a change of scene.

Imprisoned here, not daring
to peep above the shadow
line where the air presses down,

it is dark, and then a break
of light, cold and shrill, bubbles
and the shining salmon, with

their crooked jaws, flattening
the weeds with a bow wave, slide
over us like the morning.

We see the rocks about us and their peaks and ruts
until the weeds wave gently back and enclose us.

The water is bitter to us
as we wait for their return.

XVI

The crazy houses, walls as soft as cake
built by an old bridge or on a stream
(a cellar door with a boat pointing tideward
and floods on the stairway in September and March)

crazed lethal machinery spanning inlets:
beams and rafters light with age: you showed me
the murdered distilleries that mark the streams.

They persist underground and slope alongside blank high walls,
the high stacks have crumbled.

The water bubbles through gratings, the slates loosen and crash,
the flats of water in flooded streets
are dancing, bouncing with rain.

The Duke of Marlborough, the Black and Tans...

Shopfronts now reduced to a man's height,
the mark of fire and water
still stamped black on paint and plaster.

XVII SANDSTONE

The soft rock that foils the maker
that splinters in wavering faces

in layers of broken light
color of the patched river:

even in the gravel on the shore
where bone and glass are schemed
contoured to a flattened eggshape
this one wears to roughness.

It cannot forget the alleyways within
their weaknesses, their coastlines impose.

Ridged north and south it hunches
around the city
arrogant as the intersecting
lines on the compass disk.

Séamus Murphy, Died 2 October 1975

Walking in the graveyard, a maze
of angels and families
the path coils like a shaving of wood
we stop to read the names.

In time they all come around
again, the spearbearer, the spongebearer
ladder and pillar
scooped from shallow beds.

Carrying black clothes
whiskey and ham for the wake
the city revolves
white peaks of churches clockwise lifting and falling.

The hill below the barracks
the sprouting sandstone walls go past
and as always you are facing the past
finding below the old clockface

the long rambles of the spider
in the narrow bed of a saint
the names inscribed traveling
into a winter of stone.

The Last Glimpse of Erin

The coastline, a swimmer's polished shoulder heaving
on the edge of sky; our eyes make it grow:
the last glimpse, low and smooth in the sea.

We face the air, all surfaces become
sheer, one long line is growing
like a spider's navel cord: the distance

from your low shoulder lost in the quilt,
an arm thrown forward; a swimmer, your head
buried in a pillow like a wave.

The white light skirting the cloud pierces
glass riddled with small scratches and creates
the depths and cadences of a spider's web.

A man is holding his baby and laughing,
he strokes her cheek with a brownstained finger
while his wife sews a wristbutton on his other hand.

The island trimmed with waves is lost in the sea,
the swimmer lost in his dream.

"He Hangs in Shades the Orange Bright"

So quiet the girl in the room
                                    he says
it is a precarious bowl
of piled white eggs on a high shelf

against the dark wardrobe the gleam
of skin and the damp hair inclining
over her leaning shoulder fades
into dark. She leans on a hand
clutching the bedrail, her breasts pale
askew as she stands looking left
past the window towards the bright glass.
But from the window it is clear
that the dark glass reflects nothing;
brilliance of the water-bottle
spots the ceiling.

The man in the courtyard waters the roots of the trees
and birds in their cages high on the red wall sing.

She moves her head and sees
the window tall on hinges
each oblong tightly veiled. One side admits
air through a grey slatted shutter, and light
floats to the ceiling's
profound white lake.

Still the sound of water and the stripe
of blue sky and red wall,
dark green leaves and fruit, one ripe orange
                                    she says
the sheet lightning over the mountains
as I drove over the quiet plain
past the dark orange groves.

18 March 1977

Waking with a sore head
a freshly bruised shin,
forgetting the collision:
eyes open and see
with relief, my coat on a hanger.

The early light that slants
warm from the curtain illuminates
the skin of your face,
glittering all over like a lake in a light wind—
the eyelids, those fine
horizontal folds: like cliffs by a lake
layered and loaded with flowers.

When my skin was as smooth as
a jam jar of water
I looked for time in my father's eyes:
brown and green circling,
a bead of yellow under the corner
when no part of my body
was more private than a fish
going round and round in a jam jar of water.

from *The Rose Geranium*

She learned again so soon
how the body is subdued
to all the laws that rule
the acorn's fall and the erosion of tall cliffs.

Like one borne away in a dance and veiled
she dreamed of a high house with shining floors
where they squatted over stoves
and well-shod women held breath in the lift
if ever they went out or in.

They chewed into the side of the tower,
a fungus. From the night-time street
the rooms they had invaded showed—
their half-light, their droning seeped.

And the day the building fell into the street
and blood fell and bodies folded and spun
the prisoner had company:

x-ray bones of snow.
Rivers grinding south,
planes of ice bleeding at the edges downstream.

III

When she opened the egg the wise woman had given her,
she found inside some of her own hair and a tooth, still
bloody, from her own mouth.

One summer after another
the shore advanced and receded
as the boat shoved past the islands.

Dark bushy hills revolved in the path;
                          and in each
of the solid still rooms above bars,
                    the first sight
caught at an angle, the glass questioning your face.

IV

"À l'usage de M. et Mme. van Gramberen"
—the convent phrase (nothing is to be mine,
everything ours) marks the small round enclosure,
its table and bench. Distinguished
from the other old people, from the nuns' gravel
they sat in the windmill's afternoon shadow, half
hidden by a moving carthorse's huge blond rump
and quarreled over their sins for Saturday:
Examination of Conscience before Confession

prepared and calm in case one thought
struck them both, an attentive pose
eluding me now, at ten in the morning, alone
with a clean college pantry: piled rings
of glass rising, smooth as a weir.

The moment sways
tall and soft as a poplar
pointing into a lifetime of sky.

V

The precious dry rose geranium smell
comes down with spirals of sunlit dust
from the high sill: nodding stems
traveling out from the root
embrace a fistful of dusk among the leaves.

The man sitting below, his head
veiled in smoke, the face a cliff in shadow,
waits: the sun in Scorpio climbs in
dodging the fragrant leaves; and as subtly

as the eyes of two musicians touching
light strokes his hair in place.

In spite of your long horizontal twilights
there is an instant when the sun meets the sea
dividing light from dark
an hour when the shadow passes the mark on the wall
and the cloud of the rose geranium dulls your hair.

VII

Light glancing along a public-house table
stamps rings of glass like the circles left
marking the skin of water as the pebble skips.

Light catches on hands
reaching out of sleeves,
on shaded faces.

The head upright
vertical bones,
eyebrows level,
stiffening, that
image I see when I please.

I am watching the man watching the boy.

Grace, the instant overloaded, the spine
righting itself, treading water. The boy
making tea, leaning over the sink, lands
his weight on one foot, riding—
that seahorse backbone, ruffled at the hip;
the breeze lifting, filling cloth.

Sloping westward, the roads of the body,
drumlin shoulder. I will lie down
where the ivy begins its approaches,
where the weight of the body burns into the earth.

XII

So rarely we lie
as then, in darkness
a vertical gleam relieved
where the brilliance from outside
struck the glass over the hearth

(breast high, if one stood,
night lapped the bookshelves
and a dying light floated
above us, never reaching
us, our arrested embrace)

I think at once of
that amphibious
twilight, now that the year is
revisiting the spring shrine.
At my window the sharp, grey

rectangles of stone
range, parade in squares.
February light
spreading across the walls over my head
washes my room with shadows, cold until morning.

XIII

The bones wake up, reach
like tendrils for support
they feel the air in their cavities
thunder of racehorses comes to them in the earth.

And, lightly rising, they climb aloft on her shoulders.
At once her own bones are reminded—it is the same,
the pressure—the rim of the clavicle biting
as the long humerus idly swings by her side.

Empty as a diagram
the laughable straight lines
even now hold secrets
of pleasure and fatigue. She sleeps,
her head in the dish of a pelvis:
she knows how they stir beneath her.

XV

Linked by precious chains
the feathered shapes moved with her as she moved,
still descending lava stairs
between scrub and a scatter
of pines waving on the slope.
The command was, not to look
down, but she did and saw the shore:

an oval sea, with the gleam
of an iron lid raised an instant,
the rough pebbles where no boat rested
or wave stirred among the weed.

And beyond the inlet, beyond the stiff black trees
that circle the burnt-out island,
still flying, nesting, the slim grey birds
without a cry, those birds of whom
no history of shapes transformed
or grief outlived is ever told.
They flourish there, by the subterranean sea.

XVI

Because this is the age of his life
in retrospect he will name theirs
he calls now at noon to feed their cats;
and stretched on a chaise longue in the clean house
he bites one of the yellow sweet apples
wrinkling in the dish, while the female
noses his feet. The black cat watches him
from the padded rail at his elbow:
a short demanding stare;
                              he recalls
a hand that shut off day,
an eye so close to what it sought, half-blinded,
a collage of hair and upholstery.

Beyond the half-drawn curtain, past the trailing boughs
of their proper domain,
a goldfinch lights up
childhood's cramped retreats,
covenants made in
the scarce blood of berries
that dry on the twig.

The cats his shortlived witnesses.

XVII AMELIA

Remembering her half-sister Amelia, that girl
whose hips askew made every step seem upstairs
the woman at the airport tells me that from her
one spring she bought the first small car.

After that it was trains and taxis for Amelia
for years and years, while the younger lay
in the car in a leafy mews in Dublin
making love to a bald actor
her elbow tightening
linked through the steering wheel.

She tells me, this hot noisy afternoon,
that Amelia now drives a car like a cabin cruiser
in Halifax, Nova Scotia, where her husband
fishes for lobster in short ice-free summers.

I run my hand along the clean wood
and at once I am stroking the heads
of everyone in the room.
                              Looking into the grain
wavered and kinked like hairlines, what I see
is the long current of a pale ocean
softly turning itself inside out.

Palm slack as air's belly touching the sea—
I feel the muscles tugging
in the wood, shoals hauling.

I look in vain for that boat
biting its groove to the south-east,
for that storm, the knot of blindness
that left us thrashing
in steel corridors in the dark.

Beyond the open window
along the silkpacked alleys of the souq
momentary fountains and stairways
    (my hands move over the table
     feeling the spines of fish and the keels)
I look in vain at the street plan
searching for a man with hair like yours.

The Magdalene Sermon

Pygmalion's Image

Not only her stone face, laid back staring in the ferns,
but everything the scoop of the valley contains begins to move
(and beyond the horizon the trucks beat the highway.)

A tree inflates gently on the curve of the hill;
an insect crashes on the carved eyelid;
grass blows westward from the roots
as the wind knifes under her skin and ruffles it like a book.

The crisp hair is real, wriggling like snakes;
a rustle of veins, tick of blood in the throat;
the lines of the face tangle and catch, and
a green leaf of language comes twisting out of her mouth.

The Liturgy

He has been invited to perform
the very ancient ceremony, the Farewell to Fire,
and with misgivings has agreed.

The day comes and doubt comes back.
He never thought his initiation
would lead to this, he planned a quiet life
studying the epigrams incised
on millennial plaques. And that
is the reason he was asked to officiate;
the devotees in their casual search
had spotted the sacred metal in his luggage.

He stands in the September afternoon glow, balancing
the copper shells and their ritual pouch in two hands,
then clatters off down the stairs of the hostel.

They are waiting outside, the muffled band,
their boat moored and loaded
with piled blankets, crocheted shawls,
nets of mellowed fruit. Behind them,
the glitter of the estuary, the honeycomb
of cliffs riddled with sunlight.

Meanwhile the house is empty
except for the two women on the ground floor.
The latch of their room will never shut completely.
They hear the hinges of the big door closing,
they know the length of the ceremony, they know
they have just forty minutes.

History

Accept the gift
ancestral flood
parting the ground
washing the living
shearing the bank of ghosts—

these will not cauterize a wound.

The fire polluted you
with menstrual stain
dirt from forges
ashes fat and bones
from the invaders' feast.

The leaves of yellow metal
were floated to us on the stream
our grandmothers wrote in them
with reeds and vinegar—
that is a lost art.

Our history is a mountain of salt
a leaking stain under the evening cliff
it will be gone in time
grass will grow there—

not in our time.

Observations from Galileo

I

If two such bodies are to touch each other
they will touch at one point only. This is plain
though we do not know what they are, or if one
looking like a dry fist of asphalt
is in fact our tidal earth. Even so,
over all her wild complexion there is only
one point where a man is proving, with basins of water
and sun reflected on a whitewashed wall,
as the servants draw long curtains back,
that such great bodies have their currents,
they feel corruption though they spell our time.

II

But who has not seen, in a city at night,
returning home, how the moon jumps
from a gable to a high wall, keeps pace as you go
running along the rim of the wall like a cat?

Crossing

He thought his death near then, his life seemed
like a drop within him, nearly at the dregs,
the stopper lost and the air sucking it dry.

I walked in the plantation with him and his grown children
to a graceful house burnt-out, Currah Chase,
blunt on its eminence among the young spruce.

When we came to the neat locked gate
he climbed it without pausing, and we followed
his tracks to the ruin, its black windows lying

open as the ornamental water below
to the *droit de seigneur* of the visiting swans—
the breeze rising, airing the cellars.

The Pig-boy

It was his bag of tricks she wanted, surely not him:
the pipkin that sat on the flame, its emissions
transporting her so she skipped from kitchen to kitchen
sampling licks of food; she knew who had bacon
and who had porridge and tea. And she needed
the swoop of light from his torch
that wavered as she walked,
booted, through the evening fair,
catching the green flash of sheep's eyes,
the glow of false teeth in the skull:

its grotto light stroked oxters of arches,
bridges, lintels, probed cobbles of tunnels
where the world shook itself inside out like a knitted sleeve:
light on the frozen mesh, the fishbone curve, the threads
and weights.
        And as day
glittered on the skin, she stood
in the hood of a nostril and saw
the ocean gleam of his eye.

Permafrost Woman

Now, that face he coursed
beyond all the lapping
voices, through linear deserts

unfolds among peaks
of frozen sea, the wave
coiling upward its wrinkled grace.

Dumb cliffs tell their story, split and reveal
fathomed straits. The body opens its locks.

Spying the crowded
ocean graveyard, wrecks shifting
a sea mile to the west as the blow falls,

the traveler feels
his hair bend at the fresh weight
of snow, the wind is an intimate fist

brushing back strands: he stares at the wide mouth, packed
with grinding ash; the landslide of his first dream.

Street

He fell in love with the butcher's daughter
when he saw her passing by in her white trousers
dangling a knife on a ring at her belt.
He stared at the dark shining drops on the paving stones.

One day he followed her
down the slanting lane at the back of the shambles.
A door stood half open
and the stairs were brushed and clean,
her shoes paired on bottom step,
each tread marked with the red crescent
her bare heels left, fading to faintest at the top.

The Hill-town

The bus floats away on the big road and leaves her
in sunlight, the only moving thing to be seen.

The girl at her kitchen window in the ramparts
can glimpse her through a steep rift between houses.
She turns to salt the boiling water
as her mother begins to climb, dark blue in the blue shade,
past the shut doors and the open windows,
their sounds of knife and glass.
She crosses into the sun before passing
the blank shutters of the glazier's house.

He is in there, has heard her step and
paused, with the sharp tool in his hand.
He stands, his fingers pressed against the looking glass
like a man trying to hold up a falling building
that is not even a reflection now.

Their child knows where to glance, turning off the flame,
to spot her mother, a wrinkle in the light.
She remembers lying in the wide bed, three years old,
the sound of water and the gas going silent,
and the morning was in the white sieve of the curtain
where a shadow moved, her mother's body, wet patches
blotting the stretched cloth, shining like dawn.

Snow

"I thought of you then," she says, "flocking
on the edge of the same water—
the yearly walk by the banks—"
as she stood by the calm water
and the snow kept faltering past,
and past the window where a man's bare arm
reached for clothes and for matches.

"I heard him calling," she says; "I stood there, planted,
marking time." She spotted, between the branches,
how the treecreeper survives by its own rites.
The beak tapped, the wedge of time sank.

She thought of them, crowding the cold shore
with pilgrimage, like migrant birds,
their habitat a shrinking blot on the map,
the tidal ogham in their feathers keeping score.

MacMoransbridge

Although the whole house creaks from their footsteps
the sisters, when he died,
never hung up his dropped dressing gown,
took the ash from the grate, or opened his desk. His will,
clearly marked, and left in the top drawer,
is a litany of objects lost like itself.
The tarnished silver teapot, to be sold
and the money given to a niece for her music lessons,
is polished and used on Sundays. The rings and pendants
devised by name to each dear sister are still
tucked between silk scarves in his wardrobe, where he found
and hid them again, the day they buried his grandmother.
And his posthumous plan of slights and surprises
has failed—though his bank account's frozen—to dam up time.

He had wanted it all to stop,
as he stopped moving between that room
with its diaries and letters posted abroad
and the cold office over the chemist's
where he went to register deaths and births,

while the sisters went on as they do now, never
all resting at once—one of them would be
boiling up mutton-shanks for broth, or washing out blankets,
dipping her black clothes in boiled vitriol and oak-gall
(he used to see from his leafy window
shoulders bobbing at the pump like pistons).
And still the youngest goes down at night to the stream,
tending the salmon-nets at the weir
and comes home to bed as the oldest of all
can already be heard adding up small change with the servant.

Looking at the Fall

She stood again in the briar path,
her child in her hand, and looked over
where the water struck the rock, where
the divided leaf struck root, and saw
the shielded home of the spider surviving
below the curve of the fall. She said,
what will it be when summer turns
the scapula to a dry bone?

Look, don't touch, she said to the reaching child.
Across her eye a shadow fell like a door closing upstream,
a lock slipping, a high stack of water
loosed, spinning down, to slam them out of breath.

She looked again at the fall—
the rock half dry, the skein of water
crooked and white—and saw
the ribs of a candle,
the flame blown adrift,
a draught from a warped door.

She looked at the rock and saw bone
and saw the bones piled in the mountainside
and the crosswind cutting at the roots,
whistling in the dry bed of the stream.

Balloon

Let the child sleep now
the judge has finished, the papers are signed,
the cameras done flashing
on him as he held on tightly
to his lighter-than-air balloon.

Warm currents of his room
shake the flagging lost balloon, revive
a floated search, coasting
from shelf, past open door, to rest
on a dance floor, held and freed

by a loose jet of air.
Twisting the whiskered angles of toys,
of musical instruments resting,
the silk lobe flutters not quite down to earth:
a big strange fish gleams, filling the child's bed.

London

At fifty, she misses the breast
that grew in her thirteenth year
and was removed last month. She misses
the small car she drove through the seaside town
and along cliffs for miles. In London
she will not take the tube, is afraid of taxis.

We choose a random bar. She sits by me,
looking along the jacketed line of men's
lunchtime backs, drinks her vermouth.
I see her eye slide to the left;
at the counter's end sits a high metal urn.

What are you staring at? That polished curve,
the glint wavering on steel, the features
of our stranger neighbor distorted.
You can't see it from where you are.
When that streak of crooked light
goes out, my life is over.

1981

River, with Boats

Of course she does not mind sleeping
on the deep fur of the bed
beside the wide window
where the birds hop,
where the boats pass.

She can hear the hooters
down there in a greeting;
she can see a flash of the river,
a glitter on the ceiling
when the wind blows
and the high branches of trees
on the other bank
skip and bow in circles.

Only at the highest tide
the window is blocked
by the one framed eye
of a tethered coaster
swaying and tugging and flapping with the wind,
and the faces of the mariners
crowd at the glass like fishes.

The Italian Kitchen

Time goes by the book laid open
on the long marble table: my work
in the kitchen your landlord painted yellow and white.
Beyond it the glass cupboard doors: behind them now
ranged the green and yellow cups and plates
you bought in September and left behind, still in boxes.

One more of your suddenly furnished houses.
Eighteen years since we discovered, cash in hand,
anonymous, the supermarket pleasures
stacked and shinily wrapped, right
for this country, where all wipes clean,
dries fast. Or California where you are now.

No sound from the sleeper in bed upstairs.
At the hour's end I walk over to the window
looking down on the slopes. The night mist
rises off the smoky plain, reaching
the one tall pine where cones cling like mussels,
and light still plays among the branches, touching
the cold cheek of the windowpane. For now,
we are living here; I have bought blankets and firewood.

To Eilís, Agello, March 1981

Quarant' Ore

At the dark early hour
when the open door of the church
is pumping out light,
the sacristan is at work unfolding
the stacked chairs, he carries them
out of the porch, into the glow.
They spread wide like daisies,
they turn to the wide gold rose,
follow it, ranked in rings.

And still it is not day
and the morning papers are lying
dropped by gates in grey piles,
when the first pilgrims arrive,
slipping into the dark shell of the porch,
to squat on the stone—
the practiced knees doubled against the breastbone,
the elbows not interfering. They are packed
lightly as drifted rubbish in corners.
They never obscure the blazing outline of the arch
lying open for the real congregation
to roll up punctually in cars,
the knights with medals and white gloves.

A Voice

Having come this far, in response
to a woman's voice, a distant wailing,
now he thinks he can distinguish words:
   You may come in—
   You are already in.

But the wall is thornbushes, crammed, barbed.
A human skeleton, warped in a dive, is clasped
in the grip of a flowery briar. His shrinking flesh
reproves him, turns and flows
backwards like a tide.

II

Knowing it now for a trick of the light
he marches forward, takes account of
true stones and mortared walls,
downfaces the shimmer
and shakes to hear the voice humming again:

in the bed of the stream
she lies in her bones—
wide bearing hips and square
elbows. Around them lodged,
gravegoods of horsehair and an ebony peg.

"What sort of ornament is this?
What sort of mutilation? Where's
the muscle that called up the sound,
the tug of hair and the turned cheek?"
The sign persists, in the ridged fingerbone

and he hears her voice, a wail of strings.

In Rome

The Pope's musketeers are breaking their fast
on the roof above my bed. Harsh burning of kebabs
reeks down through the gap in the beams, and the retching
of their caged doves. The captain lowered some charcoal
last night; my poor girls are cooking eggs now
behind the screen. Soon they must wrap
and veil up for the street, for the hours lounging
nibbling bread in the Cardinal's front hall,
twisting to keep their heels out of sight.

Then I have time to walk, alone on the carpet
on half the floor, where we eat and sleep together.
Not even the mice scramble on the clean boards.
We keep the bell-shrine there, and the gold chasubles
for the feast day. I must not go out.
But from the egg-shaped window
I can see the girls trailing back home, with a promise.

Indeed, only an hour after the markets close
the deaf runner from the palace climbs
with two silver pieces and odd coppers.
When we were at home it would have been three sheep—
work for the troop, skinning, washing the guts,
digging the pit for the fire. When the meat was eaten,
the wool to card and spin.
I am obliged to God for inventing the city,
to the Cardinal for the sound of money,
the clipped rounds, the battered profiles:
they circle my sleep like the faces of lost kin.

J'ai mal à nos dents

i.m. Anna Cullinane (Sister Mary Antony)

The Holy Father gave her leave
to return to her father's house
at seventy-eight years of age.

When young in the Franciscan house at Calais
she complained to the dentist, *I have a pain in our teeth*—
her body dissolving out of her first mother,
her five sisters aching at home.

Her brother listened to news
five times in a morning on Radio Éireann
in Cork, as the Germans entered Calais.
Her name lay under the surface, he could not see her
working all day with the sisters,
stripping the hospital, loading the sick on lorries,
while Reverend Mother walked the wards and nourished them
with jugs of wine to hold their strength.
J'étais à moitié saoûle. It was done,
they lifted the old sisters on to the pig-cart
and the young walked out on the road to Desvres,
the wine still buzzing and the planes over their heads.

Je mangerai les pissenlits par les racines.
A year before she died she lost her French accent
going home in her habit to care for her sister Nora
(une malade à soigner une malade).
They handed her back her body,
its voices and its death.

Consolation

His wife collects the rifled
remains. The list accounted for,
his pockets emptied, their load (codes,
lists, cards, his multiplied signature)
locked up for her claiming,
it seems little was taken.
Between the pages of his passport
a copy of his deposition
typed on the day of the incident, on a loud machine
by an irritated sergeant.

She asks the nun, "But was that what killed him,
a blow on the head?" Alive,
three days ago he asked the sergeant,
"What about the blow from behind?"
"No sir, the boy just landed from above you and snatched your wallet."
"I felt it as a blow."

He was still in the weavers' alley,
turning to look past hanging cloth down an entry—
a burrow, green light at the end,
a sliver of an arch
crossed by one trickling thread,
a segment of shoulder and arm—
and his shoulder felt the force, like a wall falling.

The hospital basement is vaulted and pillared:
a wide crypt, old and clean. The nun sits down
to rifle a desk for the right form of receipt.
"It was just as if he waited for the priest to come."
"He was quite collected, he spoke sensibly."

She hears the words, the repeated story:
there was no assassination, the fire in his brain
came only from the red of the dyed cloth.
There was a pillared space when he was dying,
a voice and a response. It was not a hunt and a blow.

Fallen Tree in a Churchyard

i.m. John Jordan

The tree falls, and
the daylight searches
where once the roots
discreetly moved one way
as a blind man's hand
through a cat's coat.

The tangle, the drying clay
coating the major passages
never until now shaped
by flood or storm,
becomes finally
visible, halved
by the acute
maker of threads, tier of knots,
binder of air and earth:

we can see it now,
forked and completed.

So She Looked, in that Company

Seeing her here
I know at once who she must be.
She does not move while
the pale figures out of the anthologies
in their coarse shirts are paraded
to tell their hesitant stories
twisting the grammar of their exotic speech.

They line up as if
back to the wall were the only possible stance.
Their throats are scarred and their voices
birdlike.
         —Until the viewing is over,
the woman waits to be taken away,
then they can be heard, heartily chatting
among themselves, calling for big jugs of drink.

Chrissie

Escaped beyond hope, she climbs now
back over the ribs of the wrecked ship,
kneels on the crushed afterdeck, between gross
maternal coils: the scaffolding
surviving after pillage.
                              On the strand
the voices buzz and sink; heads can be seen
ducking into hutches, bent over boiling pans.
The trees above the sand, like guests,
range themselves, flounced, attentive.
Four notches down the sky, the sun gores the planks;
light fills the growing cavity
that swells her, that ripens to her ending.

The tide returning shocks the keel;
the timbers gape again, meeting the salty breeze;
she lies where the wind rips at her left ear,
her skirt flapping, the anchor-fluke
biting her spine; she hears
the dull sounds from the island change
to a shrill evening cry. In her head she can see them
pushing out boats, Mother Superior's shoulder to the stern
(her tanned forehead more dreadful now
than when helmeted and veiled)
                                          and she goes on fingering
in the shallow split in the wood
the grandmother's charm, a stone once shaped like a walnut,
they had never found. Salt water soaked its force:
the beat of the oars canceled its landward grace.

She clings, as once to the horned altar beside the well.

St. Mary Magdalene Preaching at Marseille

Now at the end of her life she is all hair—
a cataract flowing and freezing—and a voice
breaking loose from the loose red hair,
the secret shroud of her skin:
a voice glittering in the wilderness.
She preaches in the city, she wanders
late in the evening through shaded squares.

The hairs on the back of her wrists begin to lie down
and she breathes evenly, her elbows leaning
on a smooth wall. Down there in the piazza,
the boys are skimming on toy carts, warped
on their stomachs, like breathless fish.

She tucks her hair around her,
looking beyond the game
to the suburban marshes.

Out there a shining traps the sun,
the waters are still clear,
not a hook or a comma of ice
holding them, the water-weeds
lying collapsed like hair
at the turn of the tide;

they wait for the right time, then
flip all together their thousands of sepia feet.

The Informant

Underneath the photograph
of the old woman at her kitchen table
with a window beyond (fuchsias, a henhouse, the sea)
are entered: her name and age, her late husband's occupation
(a gauger), her birthplace, not here
but in another parish, near the main road.
She is sitting with tea at her elbow
and her own fairy cakes, baked that morning
for the young man who listens now to the tape
of her voice changing, telling the story,
and hears himself asking,
Did you ever see it yourself?
                              Once, I saw it.

Can you describe it? But the sound
takes off like a jet engine, the machine
gone haywire, a tearing, an electric
tempest. Then a stitch of silence.
Something has been lost, the voice resumes
quietly now
                    The locks
forced upward, a shift of air
pulled over the head. The face bent
and the eyes winced, like craning
to look in the core of a furnace.
The man unraveled
back to a snag, a dark thread.

Then what happens?
                              The person disappears.
For a time he stays close by and speaks
in a child's voice. He is not seen, and
you must leave food out for him, and be careful
where you throw water after you wash your feet.
And then he is gone?

He's gone, after a while.

You find this more strange than the yearly miracle
of the loaf turning into a child?
Well, that's natural, she says,
I often baked the bread for that myself.

A Whole Life

Down here it's sheltered, and the children play
rolling down the grass bank
and always roll crooked; we look up;
The temple cranes out over the hill,
seeming to fall as the wind flourishes, through
arches opening on blanks, gallops up tumbles
of crooked stairs, around pillars weathered,
sucked by every breath that's blown here since the Fall.

Never equipped with a graveyard or a kitchen midden,
there's nothing to dig, the foundations
are sand, the level flags are too smooth
to show a date; it faces every way.

—Along the skyline pass two black monks
bearing a weighty book with an iron clasp.
They march between the arches and can still be seen.

Thus, after the lessons, the warnings
from the lady with the French pleat and the colonel's cap
—*Remember, you will have only one chance*—
the skills work to perfection, the parachute spreads,
the wind is a slide conveying the graceful soldier
to a landing on soft, crusted snow.

Those People

When the four women tramp in sight
dragging their children round the corner,
all the dolls in the shop windows look askance.
The shopkeepers know these people,
they are not going to leave,
they will remain visible,
still there at three in the afternoon
when the shops are closed and the bars
shutter their darkness, they will be
out on the cobbles, beside the abandoned
slimy fountain, hardly moving at all
but showing no definite signs of sleep.
At night their campfire will glow—
they will be cooking that stew,
lifting the lid to stir it, and
the smell will blow all over
as it reeks now from their skirts.

The man at the cash register
beside the looped bead curtain says
I think myself it's the goat's milk.

The Promise

In retrospect, it is all edge;
the rivers crossed were all one river, at the edge
of a wide roughened patch, one like
the mark of a blow, a mark for life;
the road linked the twin towns, falling
in loops, like a shadow in water.

There, like a beckoning arm, a tree
ventured a rounded branch between
streetpacked façades; the air expanded,
eyes shot wider, skin responded,
fingers shuffled, hidden
pianissimo, *stroking the minted*
edge. So a grave-thief
breathes deep and bristles, if
a bare coin breaches, glinting
between pelvic rags, a profile
warm from the pocket of Constantine.

In retrospect, it was all
a prelude to the embarkation.
I watch the bones, and they begin to shine.

Where, like a welded scar, we show
where we have split and healed askew—

you rock inside your skin
your bones rock in your flesh
the full bottles in the duty free shop
rattle like bells on the soft waves.

Nothing is going to happen until we land.

The Brazen Serpent

Hair

She gets that dark red hair from her grandfather.
The morning he saw it had begun to grow
he stood clutching the marble of his bald head,
the towel still in his hand. He remembered the night
they were all shouting indoors and he was the one
left in the yard, his temple pressed against the downpipe,
aware, as the church bell struck, of the white presence of mist.

Fireman's Lift

I was standing beside you looking up
through the big tree of the cupola
where the church splits wide open to admit
celestial choirs, the fall-out of brightness.

The Virgin was spiraling to heaven,
hauled up in stages. Past mist and shining,
teams of angelic arms were heaving,
supporting, crowding her, and we stepped

back, as the painter longed to
while his arm swept in the large strokes.
We saw the work entire, and how the light

melted and faded bodies so that
loose feet and elbows and staring eyes
floated in the wide stone petticoat
clear and free as weeds.

This is what love sees, that angle:
the crick in the branch loaded with fruit,
a jaw defining itself, a shoulder yoked,

the back making itself a roof
the legs a bridge, the hands
a crane and a cradle.

Their heads bowed over to reflect on her
fair face and hair so like their own
as she passed through their hands. We saw them
lifting her, the pillars of their arms

(her face a capital leaning into an arch)
as the muscles clung and shifted
for a final purchase together
under her weight as she came to the edge of the cloud.

Parma 1963 – Dublin 1994

The Architectural Metaphor

The guide in the flashing cap explains
the lie of the land.
The buildings of the convent, founded

here, a good mile on the safe side of the border
before the border was changed,
are still partly a cloister.

This was the laundry. A mountain shadow steals
through the room, shifts by piles of folded linen.
A radio whispers behind the wall:

since there is nothing that speaks as clearly
as music, no other voice that says
hold me I'm going ... so faintly,

now light scatters, a door opens, laughter breaks in,
a young girl barefoot, a man pushing her
backwards against the hatch—

it flies up suddenly—
there lies the foundress, pale
in her funeral sheets, her face turned west

searching for the rose-window. It shows her
what she never saw from any angle but this:
weeds nested in the churchyard, catching the late sun,

herself at fourteen stumbling downhill
and landing, and crouching to watch
the sly limbering of the bantam hen

foraging between gravestones—
                         help is at hand
though out of reach:
                         the world not dead after all.

1989

The Real Thing

The Book of Exits, miraculously copied
here in this convent by an angel's hand,
stands open on a lectern, grooved
like the breast of a martyred deacon.

The bishop has ordered the windows bricked up on this side
facing the fields beyond the city.
Lit by the glow from the cloister yard at noon
on Palm Sunday, Sister Custos
exposes her major relic, the longest
known fragment of the Brazen Serpent.

True stories wind and hang like this
shuddering loop wreathed on a lapis lazuli
frame. She says, this is the real thing.
She veils it again and locks up.
On the shelves behind her the treasures are lined.
The episcopal seal repeats every coil,
stamped on all closures of each reliquary
where the labels read: *Bones
of Different Saints. Unknown.*

Her history is a blank sheet,
her vows a folded paper locked like a well.
The torn end of the serpent
tilts the lace edge of the veil.
The real thing, the one free foot kicking
under the white sheet of history.

La Corona

Since the mother took to her bed
she cannot guess how they live downstairs.
She manages her time.

The Feast of the Four Crowned Martyrs
was also her wedding day.
The relics are sewn into the hem of her shift.

The day of the eclipse
fell on the feast of St. Rita.
A flower from the Holy Thorn, brought home by pilgrims,
bleeds as dry as paper between
chasms of favored pages, riven hymns
that slice her leatherbound Manual.

Through the high window light forces its wedge
to blot out the calendar; the mountainside
flooding, the water fanned in veins, backs
against a dark cloud with a bright snake at its edge.

A daughter, hair dripping,
lands in the doorway, framed
in the glow from the votive lamp.
She dumps down tea on a tray
and is gone with a splash
muttering about paying the milkman.

The old one shuffles weathered paper
deals herself a new hand:
five cards with black borders
and the heroes', her cousins'
grey hatchet faces.

The Tale of Me

The child's teeth click against the marble.
Her ear is crushed cold against the slab,
the dredged flour almost brushed by her hair.
She traces with her eye her mother's hand.

The hand squashes flour and eggs to hide the yeast
and again it folds and wraps away
the breathing, slackening, raw loaf
that tried to grow and was twisted and turned back—

like the man in the next room
wrapped as Adam in broad leaves,
hiding under the folded mountains that fell on him
when he called them to come and cover him over.

He lies twisted around
the pain salting his belly and gut,
lies still groaning: I am not I,
my story is folded and
soured like the bread she made.

All for You

Once beyond the gate of the strange stableyard, we dismount.
The donkey walks on, straight in at a wide door
and sticks his head in a manger.

The great staircase of the hall slouches back,
sprawling between warm wings. It is for you.
As the steps wind and warp
among the vaults, their thick ribs part; the doors
of guardroom, chapel, storeroom
swing wide and the breath of ovens
flows out, the rage of brushwood,
the roots torn out and butchered.

It is for you, the dry fragrance of tea-chests
the tins shining in ranks, the ten-pound jars
rich with shriveled fruit. Where better to lie down
and sleep, along the labeled shelves,
with the key still in your pocket?

The Glass Garden

The spider's blessing on my shoulder holds me back—
a sleek trailing thread catching the light
breaks off like a hesitant voice, a breathing
silence binding, tracing me.

I've been in the orchard where
holding long crooked guns
massed men in steel caps
full to the lip with grave life
stood staring in arrested profile.

And I've been inside the house beyond the trees
cut and lying open in segments:
the morning shone straight in at the two doors
brushing the scrubbed floor, showing up
a hairline slit in the lens of my right eye,
transparent, a swimming impulse,
a thread searching upstream.

A Glass House

The joists have become transparent—
I can see what they do downstairs,
the dark blue bottle on the laundry shelf,
the label turned in to the corner.

Relaxed like the sea flower
both eyes drugged and wide
in the clear salty pool
open to the tides, I am sinking

past open globes of eyes.
I can see where the sandy floor
brushes away; a cloud floats
puffed into the shape of myself.

Crates of racing pigeons wait
rustling on a platform.
How far do I need to travel
to understand their talk?

The Water Journey

I sent the girl to the well.
She walked up the main road as far as Tell's Cross,
turned left over the stile and up the hill path.
I stood at the door to watch her coming down,
her eyes fixed on the level of the water
cushioned in her palms, wavering
like the circles of grain in wood.

She stepped neatly down on the road;
the lads on bicycles cheered as they passed her
and her fingers shook and nearly leaked and lost it.
She took her time for the last fifty yards
bringing it to the threshold and there I drank.

I said to the other sisters, each of you
will have to do the same when your day comes.
This one has finished her turn,
she can go home with her wages;
she would hardly make it as far
as the well at the world's end.

Passing Over in Silence

She never told what she saw in the wood;
there were no words for the stench,
the floated offal, the burnt patches.
She kept the secret of the woman lying
in darkness breathing hard,
a hooked foot holding her down.
She held her peace about the man who waited
beside the lettered slab. He sang:

I went into the alehouse and called for a drink,
the girl behind the bar could not speak for tears,
the drops of beer flowed down the sides of the glass;
she wept to think of the pierced head,
the tears our Savior shed.

St. Margaret of Cortona

Patroness of the Lock Hospital, Townsend Street, Dublin

She had become, the preacher hollows his voice,
a name not to be spoken, the answer
to the witty man's loose riddle, what's she
that's neither maiden, widow nor wife?

A pause opens its jaws
in the annual panegyric,
the word *whore* prowling silent
up and down the long aisle.

Under the flourishing canopy
where trios of angels mime the last trombone,
behind the silver commas of the shrine,
in the mine of the altar her teeth listen and smile.

She is still here, she refuses
to be consumed. The weight of her bones
burns down through the mountain.
Her death did not make her like this;

her eyes were hollowed
by the bloody scene: the wounds
in the body of her child's father
tumbled in a ditch. The door was locked,
the names flew and multiplied; she turned
her back but the names clustered and hung
out of her shoulderbones
like children swinging from a father's arm,
their tucked-up feet skimming over the ground.

Our Lady of Youghal

Flowing and veiling and peeled back, the tide
washed the bulk of timber
beached on the mud, so heavy
twelve horses could not pull it.

A lay brother rose at dawn, and saw it moved,
the weight melted away,
to the shore below the water gate.
He rolled it easily as far as the cloister.

At rest on the lip of weathered
rough steps and the icy pavement,
it paused among the kneeling poor
the bark still crude and whole.

It takes the blind man's fingers
blessing himself in the entry
to find the secret water treasured
in the tree's elbow; he washes his eyes and sees

a leaf cutting its way to the air
inside a tower of leaves,
the virgin's almond shrine, its ivory lids parting
behind lids of gold, bursting out of the wood.

No Clothing/No Loads/
No Spaces Allowed in the Library

You must go naked in the library.
That pure white gown
they hand you entering weighs nothing at all.
You put it on, surrender
everything but a few blank pages.
They lend you a pencil that writes and rubs clean.

The supervisor has long fair hair.
You sit underground,
she sees you on a screen, white against a window,
a marble court beyond. Her gaze sharpens,
a strand of her hair gets frozen, permanently
trapped in the woolen band the man beside her weaves.

Just so twelve years ago I went to the church
with my hair hanging down,
I left my money and keys, I was driven
in a car not my own. There was trouble
when they called us aside to sign the papers—
they wouldn't write a line till they had their fees.

We could not move, our time settled in ice.
Sharp eyes watched in the crowd:
the beggar opened his bottle of *Marie Celeste*
and waved it around; my stepfather
drew out a concealed checkbook; in the gallery
over our heads the musicians sounded a retreat.

The Bee and the Rapeseed

The spine of the mountain stretches
and the big silent machines
in the blue shadow—the pulleys,
the cribwork, chutes, their tongues and grooves
and sliding gear intact since those days—
loom and stretch, tilted in a quarry that's hemmed
by yellow fields of rape, shoving closer,
crowding even the cool air in the shaft of the mine,

while rape honey floods the plain, folding,
dripping over the sharpened ledges.
Almshouses, their lintels low for bent age,
have beehives in their gardens; the bee soars
over tall gables, flashings and ridge tiles
clenched against the sky. She rises early;
the planted avenues direct her flight.
Crests and shadows of the hills appear, crisp

as the split edge of the apple,
pure as her mind—
                              she smells
the rapeseed sharply fenced in fields.
The traces of coulter and harrow
push through the yellow sour blooms.

The native red-ass bee is there before her,
persuaded away from the cliff and heather.

A Note

There is a note of the time
the nurse went out of the room,
the water was heard flowing—
she has not forgotten the sound.
It penetrated her mind
like the deep dints under the sand
that show when the wind blows in March
hollow like eyes in masks—
the marks the locals name
where the five fingers sank.
In March she will go there again
and see them like eyes that move,
as suddenly aware
as when the dark presence
of the wild boar crossed her path
one day on the mountain road.

Home Town

The bus is late getting in to my home town.
I walk up the hill by the barracks,
cutting through alleyways that jump at me.
They come bursting out of the walls
just a minute before I began to feel them
getting ready to arch and push. Here is the house.

Nobody who knows me knows where I am now.
I have a pocketful of gravel to wake my aunt sleeping
behind the third dark window counting left over the bakery.

Here I will not be asked to repeat the story.
Between her and me and the hour of my birth
a broad stony stream is sliding
that changes its course with the floods of every spring.

"Following her coffin in a dream..."

Following her coffin in a dream
in the country of bells, his heart
waits for the signal to beat
as the cramped forearm feels for the scythe.

A herd of old men shrinks to a file
in thick coats climbing singly.
The flexed ankle turns at the top of the stile,
the foot spreads to match the weathered flagstone,

the dry throat remembers thirst
at the fasting hour, the dizzy stomach of prayer.
The hair above his collar itches,
he looks down at the cap in his fingers.

The air's profile parting waves of grass
cuts a path to the voices behind the yews;
the skin on the back of his hands tells him the way to go
like the tide returning threading the mazes of sand.

"In the year of the hurricane..."

In the year of the hurricane
the sea rose as high as the church,
the waves were hollow, like a crypt.

When they were gone, the sand blown aside,
the bounds of ancient farms
stuck up, stone on bare stone.

The high-waterline scored in rock
begins our lives again.

Below it lace of tidemarks
washed like nets, with trimming
of cork and foam, the trailing skirts

lapping and overlapping,
are shelved like the webbed shawls
of the child wrapped and cradled,
fostered after the storm.

Following

So she follows the trail of her father's coat through the fair
shouldering past beasts packed solid as books,
and the dealing men nearly as slow to give way—
a block of a belly, a back like a mountain,
a shifting elbow like a plumber's bend—
when she catches a glimpse of a shirt-cuff, a handkerchief,
then the hard brim of his hat, skimming along,

until she is tracing light footsteps
across the shivering bog by starlight,
the dead corpse risen from the wakehouse
gliding before her in a white habit.
The ground is forested with gesturing trunks,
hands of women dragging needles,
half-choked heads in the water of cuttings,
mouths that roar like the noise of the fair day.

She comes to where he is seated
with whiskey poured out in two glasses
in a library where the light is clean,
his clothes all finely laundered,
ironed facings and linings.
The smooth foxed leaf has been hidden
in a forest of fine shufflings,
the square of white linen
that held three drops
of her heart's blood is shelved
between the gatherings
that go to make a book—
the crushed flowers among the pages crack
the spine open, push the bindings apart.

Woman Shoeing a Horse

This is the path to the stile
and this is where I would stand—
the place is all thick with weeds.

I could see the line of her back and the flash of her hair
as she came from the fields at a call,
and then ten minutes wasted, all quiet

but the horse in the open air clanking his feet
until the fire was roaring and the work began,
and the clattering and dancing.

I could see by her shoulders how her breath shifted
in the burst of heat, and the wide gesture of her free arm
as she lifted the weight and clung

around the hoof. The hammer notes were flying
all urgent with fire and speed, and precise
with a finicky catch at the end—

but the noise I could not hear was the shock of air
crashing into her lungs, the depth
of the gasp as she turned with a ready hand

as the heat from the fire drew up the chimney,
the flame pressing, brushing out the last thread,
constantly revising itself upwards to a pure line.

I closed my eyes, not to see the rider as he left.
When I opened them again the sheep were inching forward,
a flock of starlings had darkened the sky.

Daniel Grose

The breach widens at every push,
the copingstone falls
to shatter the paved floor.
Then silence for three centuries
while a taste for ruins develops.

Now the military draughtsman
is training his eye
on the upright of the tower,
noting the doors that open on treetops;
he catches the light in the elder branches
rooted in the parapet, captures
the way the pierced loop keeps exactly
the dimensions of the first wounding,
holding in the same spasm the same long view
of field and river, cottage and rock
all the way to the deconsecrated
abbey of the Five Wounds.

Where is the human figure
he needs to show the scale
and all the time that's passed
and how different things are now?

No crowds engaged in rape or killing,
no marshaling of boy soldiers,
no cutting the hair of novices.
The old woman by the oak tree
can be pressed into service
to occupy the foreground.
Her feet are warmed by drifting leaves.

He stands too far away
to hear what she is saying,
how she routinely measures
the verse called the midwife's curse
on all that catches her eye, naming
the scholar's index finger, the piper's hunch,
the squint, the rub, the itch of every trade.

Vierge Ouvrante

Overhead on the ladder
a craftsman can be heard ascending
balancing the hammer and nails.

He tacks up the photographs:
how can he hold in his head all the leaves of that tree
whose roots are everywhere, whose seed
outnumbers the spawn of the ocean?

The woman in an anorak, snapped
face down in a drain, her bare arse
signaling to helicopters, hardly
finds room beside the man boldly
laid out on the stone slab
as naked as an elephant.

Mercifully in the last room
cameras are not allowed.
You have to do your best with glass and shadows
and the light shining along the passages of your skull
to capture her, to remember

the opening virgin, her petticoats
shelved like the poplars of an avenue
that slip aside until she uncovers the scars,
the marks of the ropes that chafed and held her
so she could not move or write but only commit
to the long band of memory that bound her like a silkworm's thread
the tearing, the long falling, the splashing and staining she saw.
And as she unwinds she begins to spin like a dancer against the clock
and in one minute the room is full of the stuff, sticky,

white as a blue-bleached sheet in the sun—
till there is nothing left of the darkness you need
for the *camera obscura*,
only the shining of the blank chronicle of thread.

Man Watching a Woman

The sound of everything folding into sleep,
a sense of being nowhere at all,
set him on his way (traffic far off, and wind
in tall trees) to a back gate, a dark yard.
A path goes past the bins, the kitchen door,
switches to a gravel walk by the windows
lit softly above the privet hedge.
He stops and watches. He needs to see this:

a woman working late in the refectory,
sewing a curtain, the lines of her face
dropping into fatigue, severity, age,
the hair falling out of its clasp at her poll.
The hands are raised to thread the needle,
the tongue moves behind her lips.
He cannot see the feet or shoes, they are trapped
in toils of cloth. He is comforted.

He can move on, while the night combs out
long rushing sounds into quiet,
on to the scene, the wide cafés—
trombone music over polished tables.
He will watch the faces behind the bar, tired girls,
their muscles bracing under breakers of music
and the weight of their balancing trays, drinks, ice and change.

The Pastoral Life

You remember how often we stopped
at that corner house to drink lemonade in the kitchen
and cycled on down to the harbor
the breeze filling our skirts.

But years later I passed their door,
suddenly taking the mountain road.
I labored up between rocks
until when I turned east to the plain I heard

'the corncrake in the shining grass.
The horses froze in troops of seven or eight
and a dull sound carried all that distance,
the bells around the necks of the leaders.

Will I ever go back? After the years I spent there
depending on idleness that never let me down—
I waited for the wind to blow hairs in at my door
carrying the story of the breed, for the right light
to show up the printing of muscle under the hide?
Could I go back after vesting my years

and leaving just once in November until the spring
when I found the plain blackened by fire
and staggered over bones too heavy for me to bury,

—like finding a friend's ashes evenly shed
on the open page of a book?
                         I hear now, and believe it,
the grass has grown back,
                         the horses are breeding there again.

The Party Wall

We were all still living at home then,
in the house with the fancy grilles
and the tall iron gates that let us out
gliding to business and back at night for our tea.
We rose one morning to find the garden
drifted and crisped with stiff white feathers.
They shone bluish against the red brick walls,
as they shifted and settled in the draught from the street.

We were not shocked at all until the next day
when the aerial photographs were published
showing the house that backed against ours
but looked away across the Avenue
visited the same, its roof and courtyards
blessed with angeldown and cobalt shadows.

The tenants had my grandfather's name.
I went on my bicycle to see Father Deveney
in his room in the old priests' home.
We sat at the window looking towards Mount Desert
and he ate sweets and told me he remembered
when that house too had been part of his parish.
But he had never been told my aunt's story
about all the trouble over building the party wall.

That Summer

So what did she do that summer
when they were all out working?

If she moved she felt a soft rattle
that settled like a purseful of small change.
She staggered through the quiet of the house,
leaned on a flowering doorpost
and went back inside from the glare
feeling in her skirt pocket the skin on her hands,
never so smooth since her fourteenth year.

One warm evening they were late;
she walked across the yard with a can,
watered a geranium and kept on going
till she came to the ridge looking over the valley
at the low stacked hills, the steep ground
between that plunged like a funnel of sand.
She couldn't face back home, they came for her
as she stood watching the hills breathing out and in,
their dialogue of hither and yon.

The Secret

Instead of burning the book or getting its value
they hid it and were silent, even at home,
so that the history of that lost year
remained for each one her own delusion.
As the memory faded they had to live.
No one would buy their blood, but they sold
their hair, the milk from their breasts,
their signatures on slips of raveled paper,
the grazing as far as the drawing-room windows
and at last the fresh fine grass
that had started to grow under the first arch
of the bridge beside the burnt-out paper mill.

A Witness

Can I be the only one alive
able to remember those times?
What keeps them from asking the others?

As I start on my dinner of dogfish and cockles
a draught blows the hinges and one of them shuffles
in on the floor to sound me about our troubles.

Though he's nearly as old as myself the grey hags in the corner
are beginning to watch his motions
as he loses his pencil and the page in his notebook.

I tell him about the day the mouse tumbled
in the one jar of oil and my mother shouting
at the Yank captain that all her geese were stolen.

I fix my eye on the mountain across the valley
where we all came from and on the one cloud stalling
clamped on the wild shelf, that will not move away.

Beyond the walls I can hear the children playing
in the riverbed. If I could tell what they are crying
it would lighten my darkness like knowing the language of birds.

On the Day

Why is the room opened,
the man half-seen in shirtsleeves
with a click of forks being counted—

the glasses are lined on trays;
I cannot speak the reason
I am combing out the children's hair
dragging teeth down through silence:

because there is no time,
the fanned hand of cards is banged shut,
the melodeon's slow air tumbled and shrugged
is boxed up small in an instant and kicked
out of sight, under the bench in the kitchen.

A Posting

You are reaching me in translation,
a voice with no taste or weight,
in the tones of the hand-tinted early
print of the Café du Port: palm trees,
two men in white djellabas gravely smoking,
a light struggling to climb around
the bruised edges of a cloud,

a shadow burnt into the earth.
At the sound of the voice the sea is gone
the beach a rock-salty rainbow
the flat bay a sudden gulf, even crabs
shuffled out of sight, even the word
brushed out that would name the starshaped
creature that clings to a rock shaped like a skull.

A Hand, A Wood

I

After three days I have to wash—
I am prizing you from under my nails
reluctantly, as time will deface
the tracks, their branching sequence,
the skill of the left and the right hand.

Your script curls on the labels of jars,
naming pulses in the kitchen press.
The dates you marked in the diary come and pass.

II

The wet leaves are blowing, the sparse
ashes are lodged under the trees in the wood
where we cannot go in this weather.
The stream is full and rattling,
the hunters are scattering shot—
the birds fly up and spread out.

I am wearing your shape
like a light shirt of flame;
my hair is full of shadows.

Studying the Language

On Sundays I watch the hermits coming out of their holes
into the light. Their cliff is as full as a hive.
They crowd together on warm shoulders of rock
where the sun has been shining, their joints crackle.
They begin to talk after a while.
I listen to their accents, they are not all
from this island, not all old,
not even, I think, all masculine.

They are so wise, they do not pretend to see me.
They drink from the scattered pools of melted snow:
I walk right by them and drink when they have done.
I can see the marks of chains around their feet.

I call this my work, these decades and stations—
because, without these, I would be a stranger here.

The Girl Who Married
the Reindeer

The Crossroads

I have been at the crossroads now
all the time without leaving
since the afternoon of Shrove Tuesday.

They brought me the blessed ashes
wrapped in tissue paper.

When I woke on Palm Sunday
the palm branches had been left
on the damp stones of the stile.

I heard them at Easter
across the ploughed fields,

and the little girls came and stood
a short way off, to show me
their embroidered dancing costumes.

Now it is a long time to the Feast of the Assumption,
when my mother will come

to collect me in her pony and trap
and we will go calling on all our cousins
and take tea and sherry in their parlors.

Anchoress

In the last season, she changed her ways.
The pilgrim would find only
the mossgrown window beside the church porch
and through it at times a loaf and water were passed.

A few words, a command. Yes she knew who was there,
she still prayed for them all by name. I remember
when she would give me an hour of her visions,
when she would levitate—she was always deaf—
when thin pipe music resounded beyond the grilles.

Sunday

I can't go there, but I know just how it will be.

The children will be running round and round
the house, landing to snatch a bite of food
while the couples are keeping time with knife and fork
at a table under the wisteria.

A long time later the young ones will have come to rest
in a wide half-circle which is complete
because the ducks will also have come back
with two rows of ducklings and will be all
coiling their necks to sleep under the terrace.

I can't be there, I have to hear the chestnut choir
singing in the mountain convent where they won't remember me,
but all the same, this autumn,
I am going to hear the office they sing on that Sunday
at vespers, before the longest vigil of the year.

The Chestnut Choir

All the way up the mountain
boys were breaking branches of chestnuts.
The leaves scattered on the road.
When she stopped for a hot brandy
the bar was warm, the windows misted over,
a small girl, on her way to bed,
her dolly under her elbow, crouched
staring into the wood stove's flaming center.

Outside again, her steps crunched on frosted gravel,
the trees faded into mountainside,
and still it was not dark.

The convent was close at hand,
the chapel door half-open.
She let herself in to a box pew at the back
and closed the latch. The voices had begun,
a long tutti wrapping
the walls in layers of sound.
The alto coasted and crawled,
the words were sharpened as the last light fell away:

Behold how wide are the doors
that open beneath the furnace
where the flame dives under the stone…

She leaned her cheek against the wall and the sound
came to join her, flinching in her teeth.
Then there was silence, and the two candle flames
flickered, reflected in wood. She knew
they were still there while she,
the wanderer, was free to be away.
The bar would be shut, and some beast
was snuffling outside,
but she got up and left them to their vigil.

The Angel in the Stone

Trampled in the causeway, the stone the builders passed over
calls out: "Bone of the ranked heights, from darkness
where moss and spiders never venture.
You know what ways I plumbed, past what hard threshold;

"You see our affliction, you know
how we were made and how we decay. At hand,
when the backbone splintered in the sea tide, you have heard
the twang of the waves breaking our bones.

"You look down where the high peaks are ranging,
you see them flickering like flames—
they are like a midge dancing at evening.

"Give me rest for one long day of mourning;
let me lie on the stone bench above the treeline
and drink water for one whole day."

The Cloister of Bones

I begin from the highest point,
best of all a bell tower.

I see the tops of heads, cobbles,
terraces all scuttling down
as if they hunted something buried
between ledges where tables are set in the morning,
under plants that grow over walls and pergolas,
the slopes of sheds, the stashed pruning shears,
under the measured walk of cats.

I am searching for a shape, a den, watching
for the cloistering blank of a street wall,
a dark reticence of windows
banked over an inner court,
especially rooves, arched and bouncing
naves; a corseted apse,
and always, even if the chapel sinks
deep inside, lit from a common well,
I search for hints of doors inside doors,
a built-in waiting about
of thresholds and washed floors,
an avid presence demanding flowers and hush.

If I guess right I hope for
a runner of garden, the right length
for taking a prayer book for a walk,
a small stitching of cemetery ground,
strict festivals, an hour for the tremble
of women's laughter, corners for mile-high panics:

and to find the meaning of the Women's Christmas.

Peace in the Mountains

The first day I saw this town
I came down the mountain road
past the old border post, closed now.
The road signs were in two languages
and the deer were feeding, away
on the far side of the valley,
pausing and inching forward like photographers.
I slowed and paused and let the car slide forward
again, the engine off and the gears loose,
braking and pausing all the way
as far as the first houses and walled gardens.

The wind blew steadily, brushing
every scrap of paper across the square.
There were rags of many colors
bundled and packed on the trucks
in the railway siding. A gypsy woman lay
where she had been struck down beside the bridge.
The ambulance stood by. The money changers
had closed up their shops for the day.

The same as today, the rushing grey river
tore downhill past the factory. Somewhere two streets away
it was Saturday and the immigrant weddings were feasted
behind garden walls with sweet almond milk and loud music.

A Stray

When I heard the voice on the radio
all of a sudden announcing the captives were free
I was holding my young cousin
forcibly down with two arms
gripping him back from the street
where he wanted to flatten himself
under the wheels of the cars.
I waited for the shot to work
and tried to make out what he had been wearing
half-recognizing shreds of denim,
an old velvet shirt of my own.

Next week the men were back
bigger than we remembered
sitting shakily in the kitchen—
the table a midden of crumbs and documents—
getting up in the long silences
to carry a cup to the sink
and wash it very carefully.

He stayed upstairs all May.

In June when the raspberries were in
they started to help with the picking
and after that the apples—
they spent days up the ladders
and let us get on with the cooking.
We sat long evenings outside.
But he would not work in the orchard
or eat with us at meals.

And so it remained, long after
we were used to the loud voices
hollowing from the fields—
he jumped when he heard them.
You'd find him an odd time smoking
in the courtyard by the bins
at the foot of the steep back stairs

and our liberation never
reached him. He lived on
like the last of a whole people
astray on a lost domain
bearing all their privations:
no gin and tonic, no
aspirin, just willow tea.
No tin-openers, no mules, no buses,
no Galician, no Methodists,
no fruit but rotten powdery imploded oranges,
no news from the prison cells.

Jesse

As you lie in sleep there grows like a lung inflating
a tree out of your navel, enlarging and toppling
into its perfection when the leaves and the fruit are soft as air,
are drenched like capillaries, and as they swell
they become transparent and fade away:

the true tree of knowledge which is good for nothing
but to grow out of your navel like a family tree
that each son and daughter carries the seed of,
that will grow some time and flourish and be gone.

They are able to give you only the light that passes through the leaves,
no lasting fruit at all.

In Her Other House

In my other house all the books are lined on shelves
and may be taken down in a curious mood.
The postman arrives with letters to all the family,
the table is spread and cleared by invisible hands.

It is the dead who serve us, and I see
my father's glass and the bottle of sour stout at hand
guarding his place (so I know it cannot be real;
the only boy with six sisters never learned

to set a table, though books lined up at his command).
In this room with a fire, books, a meal and a minute
when everyone is out of sight washing their hands,
a man comes through the door, shedding his coat;

he turns like a dancer before it touches the ground,
retrieving a lily from somewhere. Where he has been,
you turn out your pockets every time a door is opened;
but the flower has traveled with him and he is in safe hands—

On the shelf a letter for him flashes a wide bright stamp.
He mutters once more, *Here goes, in the name of God*—
women's voices sound outside, he breathes deeply and quickly
and returns to talk to the fire, smiling and warming his hands—
in this house there is no need to wait for the verdict of history
and each page lies open to the version of every other.

In Her Other Ireland

It's a small town. The wind blows past
the dunes, and sands the wide street.
The flagstones are wet, in places thick with glass,
long claws of scattering light.
The names are lonely, the shutters blank—
no one's around when the wind blows.

The mistress of novices has sent all the novices
upstairs into the choir to practice
the service for deliverance from storms and thunder.
Their light dapples the sharkskin windows,
the harmonium pants uphill,
the storm plucks riffs on the high tower.

And on the fair green the merry-go-round
whistles and whirls. The old man has joined
his helper on the plinth. He calls his son
to throw him a rope, and watch for a loosening
strut or a pelmet or the whole wheel
spinning lifting and drifting and crashing.

But it spins away, grinding up speed,
growling above the thunder. The rain
has begun again; the old man's helper,
darkfaced with a moustache, holds on.
They try to slow it with their weight,
calling to the youngster to hang on the rope;

it's a small town, a small town;
nowhere to go when the wind blows.

The Girl Who Married the Reindeer

I

When she came to the fingerpost
she turned right and walked as far as the mountains.

Patches of snow lay under the thorny bush
that was blue with sloes. She filled her pockets.
The sloes piled into the hollows of her skirt.
The sunset wind blew cold against her belly
and light shrank between the branches
while her feet shifted, bare,
while her hands raked in the hard fruit.

The reindeer halted before her and claimed the sloes.
She rode home on his back without speaking,
holding her rolled-up skirt,
her free hand grasping the wide antlers
to keep her steady on the long ride.

II

Thirteen months after she left home
she traveled hunched on the deck of a trader
southwards to her sister's wedding.
Her eyes reflected acres of snow,
her breasts were large from suckling,
there was salt in her hair.

They met her staggering on the quay;
they put her in a scented bath,
found a silk dress, combed her hair out.

How could they let her go back to stay
in that cold house with that strange beast?
So the old queen said, the bridegroom's mother.

They slipped a powder in her drink,
so she forgot her child, her friend,
the snow and the sloe gin.

III

The reindeer died when his child was ten years old.
Naked in death his body was a man's,
young, with an old man's face and scored with grief.

When the old woman felt his curse she sickened,
she lay in her tower bedroom and could not speak.
The young woman who had nursed her grandchildren nursed her.

In her witch time she could not loose her spells
or the spells of time, though she groaned for power.
The nurse went downstairs to sit in the sun. She slept.
The child from the north was heard at the gate.

IV

Led by the migrating swallows
the boy from the north stood in the archway
that looked into the courtyard where water fell,
his arm around the neck of his companion—
a wild reindeer staggered by sunlight.
His hair was bleached, his skin blistered.
He saw the woman in wide silk trousers
come out of the door at the foot of the stair,
sit on a cushion, and stretch her right hand for a hammer.
She hammered the dried broad beans one by one,
while the swallows timed her, swinging side to side:
the hard skin fell away, and the left hand
tossed the bean into the big brass pot.
It would surely take her all day to do them all.
Her face did not change though she saw the child watching.

A light wind fled over them
as the witch died in the high tower.
She knew her child in that moment:
his body poured into her vision
like a snake pouring over the ground,
like a double mouthed fountain of two nymphs,
the light groove scored on his chest
like the meeting of two tidal roads, two oceans.

Translation

for the reburial of the Magdalenes

The soil frayed and sifted evens the score—
there are women here from every county,
just as there were in the laundry.

White light blinded and bleached out
the high relief of a glance, where steam danced
around stone drains and giggled and slipped across water.

Assist them now, ridges under the veil, shifting,
searching for their parents, their names,
the edges of words grinding against nature,

as if, when water sank between the rotten teeth
of soap, and every grasp seemed melted, one voice
had begun, rising above the shuffle and hum

until every pocket in her skull blared with the note—
allow us now to hear it, sharp as an infant's cry
while the grass takes root, while the steam rises:

    washed clean of idiom • the baked crust
    of words that made my temporary name •
    a parasite that grew in me • that spell
    lifted • I lie in earth sifted to dust •
    let the bunched keys I bore slacken and fall •
    I rise and forget • a cloud over my time.

Bessboro

This is what I inherit—
it was never my own life,
but a house's name I heard
and others heard as warning
of what might happen a girl
daring and caught by ill luck:
a fragment of desolate
fact, a hammer-note of fear—

but I never saw the place.
Now that I stand at the gate
and that time is so long gone
it is their absence that rains,
that stabs right into the seams
of my big coat, settling
on my shoulder, in pointed
needles, crowding the short day.

The white barred gate is closed,
the white fence tracks out of sight
where the avenue goes, rain
veils distance, dimming all sound
and a half-drawn lace of mist
hides elements of the known:
gables and high blind windows.
The story has moved away.

The rain darns into the grass,
blown over the tidal lough
past the isolated roof
and the tall trees in the park;
it gusts off to south and west;
earth is secret as ever:
the blood that was sown here flowered
and all the seeds blew away.

Troubler

Did she know what she was at
when she slipped past the garden door
to palm the rolled notes from the teapot,

or later that night when she pasted
the letter at the back of Hall's *Algebra*
and pierced the date with a needle?

So quickly the instant slid back
in the haystack, pressed by its fellows—
she spent the rest of the evening

grinning on a sofa by the hour.
The photographs show her all flounces,
engrossed, a glass in her hand,

but the others' eyes are like foxes' in torchlight;
she surely knew what she was starting: a ruffle
that probed like wind in a northern garden.

In her dreams it's not that she recalls them
but they come, the treasures of time
lying packed like a knife in a garter

or scattered among the leaves.
She hears the notes whistled on the half-landing
just as the sweeping hand crowds the hour.

From an Apparition

Where did I see her, through
which break in the cloud, the woman
in profile, a great eye like a scared horse?

Seated at a till, her right hand moving,
the fingers landing precisely as if
they stopped notes on a lute, it seemed

that her other hand protected something fragile.
Then she half sprang to her feet, a captive warding off,
and the long swathe of silk she wore began to shift

flowing away like dye in water, but still she stood
cramped, and the sliding web lapped against the window
so I knew I was looking at a window,

the silk text building against the glass
in flaps and folds of yellow and arctic blue,
and bottle-dark green until the pane darkened
and closed like a big fringed eyelid into sleep.

The Crevasse

He lay plunged in the funnel of a beanbag,
the glass in his hand as deep as a fjord.
The other went out to answer the telephone,

leaving both doors open so he could see
a left leg, a left arm and half a ribcage
but no hand. On the far wall, glazed and framed,

a right shoulder and arm crushing flowers
against a breast. He reached for the bottle again,
and all the vertical lines of the house moved

a little forward, and left. They dangled and waltzed,
hanging brittle, ready to crash and split
every straight chair in the room, leaving the halves

to hop away two-legged, leaving
the walls of the house wedged open
to the four winds and the polar light.

Autun

As I drove away from the sepulchre of Lazarus,
while the French cows looked sadly out
under the wet branches of Berry,
I could hear other voices drowning
the Grande Polonaise on the radio:

Remember us, we have traveled as far
as Lazarus to Autun,
and have not we too been dead and in the grave
many times now, how long at a stretch
have we had no music but the skeleton tune
the bones make humming, the knuckles warning each other
to wait for the pause and then the long low note
the second and third fingers of the left hand
hold down like a headstone.

How often was I taken apart,
the ribs opened like a liquor press,
and for decades I heard nothing from my shoulders—
my hair flying, at large like a comet—
how often reconstructed,
wrapped and lagged in my flesh, and again
mapped and logged, rolled up and put away
safely, for ever.

On the mornings of my risings
I can hardly see in the steam.
But I know I arise like the infant
that dances out of the womb
bursting with script,
the copious long lines,
the redundant questions of childhood.
She fills the ground and the sky
with ranked and shaken banners,
the scrolls of her nativity.
I stammer out music that echoes like hammers.

Crossing the Loire

I saluted the famous river as I do every year
turning south as if the plough steered,
kicking, at the start of a new furrow, my back
to the shady purple gardens with benches under plum trees
by the river that hunts between piers and sandbanks—

I began threading the long bridge, I bowed my head
and lifted my hands from the wheel for an instant of trust,
I faced the long rows of vines curving up the hillside
lightly like feathers, and longer than the swallow's flight,
my road already traced before me in a dance

of three nights and three days,
of sidestepping hills and crescent lights blinding me
(if there was just a bar counter and ice and a glass, and a room upstairs:
but it rushed past me and how many early starts before
the morning when the looped passes descend to the ruined arch?)

She came rising up out of the water, her eyes were like sandbanks
the wrinkles in her forehead were like the flaws in the mist
(maybe a long narrow boat with a man lying down
and a rod and line like a frond of hair dipping in the stream)
she was humming the song about the estuary, and the delights
of the salt ocean, the lighthouse like a summons; and she told me:

The land will not go to that measure, it lasts, you'll see
how the earth widens and mountains are empty, only
with tracks that search and dip, from here to the city of Rome
where the road gallops up to the dome as big as the sun.

You will see your sister going ahead of you
and she will not need to rest, but you must lie
in the dry air of your hotel where the traffic grinds before dawn,
the cello changing gear at the foot of the long hill,

and think of the story of the suitors on horseback
getting ready to trample up the mountain of glass.

An Alcove

What is it, in the air or the walls
hunched over me, defending
four stiffbacked chairs caught off guard,
the knitting curled in its bag
on the low shelf by the dead fire?
The stray cat's tail twitches on the window sill,
the garden is a patch of frozen grass.

In these rooms every stitch, step and
edge of a tile is the same age, is wearing
away at the same rate, like an old lady
who brings out the sherry because tea means trouble
but has not barred her door.

There are porched crannies, for waiting in while the doctor is with her,
and the kind of book one reads in such emergencies,
with mauve and brown pictures, Paolo and Francesca
coiled like the wisteria's double trunk
in the one safe place, an alcove in the wind.

After Leopardi's Storm

The sky clears, and at the top of the street
I can hear the hen giving out her litany,
the stream rattling down the slope
in its tunnel of broom.
                              The lacemaker now
stands at her window singing,
her hand clutching her work, a cloudy ruffle
wavering its fins in the watery breeze.

Her pale face like the sky
slowly fills up with light, and spokes of light
burst from the deep hooded clump of thunder, departing.

Reflected light lies about everywhere.
Like birds we approach, to sip and splash
at the edges of our watery nature, no more—

an ordinary festival that cannot be foreseen
displays the original spindle
that never came loose, never turned,
but stayed until the long hours wrapped the stem,
now dark, now bright, an overlapping of wonders
each one confounding the last.

This afternoon salvation claims
our whole attention, like grief,
entirely here, on this side of the mountain
where the single life is lived, the backbone
upright, bracing for the next surprise.

Tower of Storms, Island of Tides

The founder of the lighthouse is not here.
She walks through other streets, pausing at a café
to smoke a cigar and check the news and the forecast.

She could not stay for ever in the blinding spray
watching the sailors being blown on to the rocks,
listening to the rain like a long thrill on the snare:

she paid for the pilot and the camera that photographed
the bones hanging on the cliff face on the one day of the year
that catches them in the northeast light between pleats of mist.

They flew on then to the islands further west
where sandy shores offered a landing place:
one sheltered field, an empty house, salt pastures.

To live there would call for another skill, as fine
as judging the set of milk for cheese,
a belief in the wisdom of a long view from one window.

Water came swimming inward as the tide turned.
They saw far off a stranded dog rushing madly around
a dry patch of sand that was getting smaller and smaller.

It dashed off into the water, then back to its island
which by now had almost disappeared.

The Bend in the Road

This is the place where the child
felt sick in the car and they pulled over
and waited in the shadow of a house.
A tall tree like a cat's tail waited too.
They opened the windows and breathed
easily, while nothing moved. Then he was better.

Over twelve years it has become the place
where you were sick one day on the way to the lake.
You are taller now than us.
The tree is taller, the house is quite covered in
with green creeper, and the bend
in the road is as silent as ever it was on that day.

Piled high, wrapped lightly, like the one cumulus cloud
in a perfect sky, softly packed like the air,
is all that went on in those years, the absences,
the faces never long absent from thought,
the bodies alive then and the airy space they took up
when we saw them wrapped and sealed by sickness
guessing the piled weight of sleep
we knew they could not carry for long:
this is the place of their presence: in the tree, in the air.

The Horses of Meaning

Let their hooves print the next bit of the story:
release them, roughmaned
from the dark stable where
they rolled their dark eyes, shifted and stamped—

let them out, and follow the sound, a regular clattering
on the cobbles of the yard, a pouring round the corner
into the big field, a booming canter.

Now see where they rampage,
and whether they are suddenly halted
at the check of the line westward
where the train passes at dawn—

If they stare at land that looks white in patches
as if it were frayed to bone (the growing light
will detail as a thickening of small white flowers),
can this be the end of their flight?
The wind combs their long tails, their stalls are empty.

A Capitulary

Now in my sleep I can hear them beyond the wall,
a chapterhouse growl, gently continuous:
the sound the child heard, waking and dozing again
all the long night she was tucked up in the library
while her father told his story to the chaplain
and then repeated it before the bishop.

She heard his flat accent, always askew
responding to the Maynooth semitones,
a pause, and then the whisper of the scribe
sweeping up the Latin like dust before a brush,
lining up the ablatives, a refined
countrywoman's hiss, and the neuter scrape of the pen.

I feel the ticking of their voices and remember how
my sister before she was born listened for hours
to my mother practicing scales on the cello;
a grumble of thick string, and then climbing
to a high note that lifted
    that lifted its head
        like a seal—
to a high note that lifted its head like a seal in the water.

Inheriting the Books

They've come and made their camp
within sight, within slingshot range,
a circle of bulked shapes
dark inside like wagons.
There are fires like open eyes.
I watch the billows of smoke,
the dark patches, hallucinating
herds and horses.

Who is that in flashing garments
bowing to the earth over and over,
is it a woman or a child?
In the wedge of the valley by the stream
what food are they cooking, what names have they
for washing the dead, for the days of the week?

The long rope has landed, the loose siege hemming me.
In whatever time remains, I will not have the strength to depart.

At My Aunt Blánaid's Cremation

In the last dark side chapel
the faces in the dome
are bending down like nurses
who lift, and fix, and straighten
the bed that's always waiting,
the last place you'll lie down.

But your face looks away now,
and we on your behalf
recall how lights and voices
and bottles and wake glasses
were lined up like the cousins
in a bleached photograph.

We carry this back to the city
since the past is all we know—
we remember the snake called Patrick,
warm in his Aran sleeves—
the past keeps warm, although
it knits up all our griefs:
a cold start in our lives.

Agnes Bernelle, 1923–1999

There is no beast I love better than the spider
that makes her own new center every day
catching brilliantly the light of autumn,

that judges the depth of the rosemary bush
and the slant of the sun on the brick wall
when she slings her veils and pinnacles.

She crouches on her knife edge, an ideogram combining·
the word for *tools* with the word for *discipline*,
ready for a lifetime of cold rehearsals;

her presence is the syllable on the white wall,
the hooked shadow. Her children are everywhere,
her strands as long as the railway line in the desert

that shines one instant and the next is doused in dust.
If she could only sing she would be perfect, but
in everything else she reminds me of you.

Borders

for John McCarter

I am driving north to your wake, without a free hand.
I must start at the start, at the white page in my mind.
I no longer own a ribbed corset of rhymes;
I am the witch who stands one-legged, masking one eye.

Passed under the soldiers' lenses at Aughnacloy,
I remember how often you crossed the map in a toil
of love (like Lir's daughter driven to the Sea of Moyle
by spells) from Dublin to Portadown or Armagh to Donegal.

So I leap over lines that are set here to hold and plan
the great global waistline in sober monoglot bands,
I follow the road that follows the lie of the land
crossing a stream called *Fairy Water*, to come to the bridge at Strabane.

A Wave

When is the wave's return?
Everything is still now,
the surface is tight and crawling.

It moves as it is drawn by the future tense
muttering like a crowd with a rumor of quarrels,
piled over a reef of glossaries.

Withdrawing it hauled away pebbles, hammering, dumping
on open mouths, boulders flattening words.
So the words are there, but stopped. When the wave comes back

drowning the watchman's brazier
and the macaronic street cries,
it will flow over all the names.

Words will be there but already,
written in the new cursive,
they waver like flourishes at the edge of a tide,

a repeating film and ripple,
clear like thin ice, displaying
a precious mosaic of sand.

The weights are buried,
the cobbles of the woodyard
sunk with their splinters deep as ballast.

The voice of the wave will be all
we will be expected to understand.

Gloss/Clós/Glas

Look at the scholar, he has still not gone to bed,
raking the dictionaries, darting at locked presses,
hunting for keys. He stacks the books to his oxter,
walks across the room as stiff as a shelf.

His nightwork, to make the price of his release:
two words, as opposite as *his* and *hers*
which yet must be as close
as the word *clós* to its meaning in a Scots courtyard
close to the spailpín ships, or as close as the note
on the uilleann pipe to the same note on the fiddle—
as close as the grain in the polished wood, as the finger
bitten by the string, as the hairs of the bow
bent by the repeated note—
                                        two words
closer to the bone than the words I was so proud of,
embrace and *strict* to describe the twining of bone and flesh.

The rags of language are streaming like weathervanes,
like weeds in water they turn with the tide, as he turns
back and forth the looking-glass pages, the words
pouring and slippery like the silk thighs of the tomcat
pouring through the slit in the fence, lightly,
until he reaches the language that has no word for *his*,
no word for *hers*, and is brought up sudden
like a boy in a story faced with a small locked door.
Who is that he can hear panting on the other side?
The steam of her breath is turning the locked lock green.

The Sun-fish

To Niall Woods and Xenya Ostrovskaia, Married in Dublin on 9 September 2009

When you look out across the fields
and you both see the same star
pitching its tent on the point of the steeple—
that is the time to set out on your journey,
with half a loaf and your mother's blessing.

Leave behind the places that you knew:
all that you leave behind you will find once more,
you will find it in the stories;
the sleeping beauty in her high tower
with her talking cat asleep
solid beside her feet—you will see her again.

When the cat wakes up he will speak in Irish and Russian
and every night he will tell you a different tale
about the firebird that stole the golden apples,
gone every morning out of the emperor's garden,
and about the King of Ireland's Son and the Enchanter's Daughter.

The story the cat does not know is the Book of Ruth
and I have no time to tell you how she fared
when she went out at night and she was afraid,
in the beginning of the barley harvest,
or how she trusted to strangers and stood by her word:

you will have to trust me, she lived happily ever after.

A Bridge Between Two Counties

The long bridge
stretched between two counties
so they could never agree
how it should be kept

standing at all
(in the mist in the darkness
neither bank could be seen
when the three-day rain

the flood waters
were rising below).
On that day I looked
where the couple walked

a woman a small child
the child well wrapped
becoming less visible
as they dodged left

then right, weaving
between the barrels and the planks
placed there to slow the traffic
and something came

a brown human shape
and the woman paused and passed
the child's hand
to a glove and a sleeve

and very slowly
at first they moved away, were gone,
there was the mist,
the woman stood and seemed

to declare something
to the tide rocking below
and for the second time
in all my life I saw

the dry perfect leaf
memory stamped in its veins
the promise I heard
Val Kennedy making

at my sister's funeral
in his eightieth year: *She will live
forever in my memory*. So her words
floated out on the water consonants

hardly visible in the mist vowels
melting and the scatter of foam
like the pebble damage
on a sheet of strong glass.

I watched the woman,
memory holding the bridge in its place,
until the child could reach the far side
and the adjoining county.

The Witch in the Wardrobe

And so she opened the plank door
where the dry palm branches had always
perched, balancing lightly,
pegged over the architrave;
she swam at once inside a fluent pantry,
a grange of luxury. The silk scarves
came flying at her face like a car wash,
then brushed her cheeks and shoulders coolly down—
the fur slid over her skin, oiled and ready,
and a cashmere sleeve whispered, probing her ear,
"We were here all along like an engine idling,
warm, gentle and alert: what will you do now?"

But when she closed her eyes to feel it closer
their swatch of sublime purples
intensely swooping and spinning
dived past her cooing like pigeons—
their prickling mauve inside her stretched eyelids—
the bridge was gone and beyond it
she could no longer see
her body, its flesh without stain, its innocent skin.

On Lacking the Killer Instinct

One hare, absorbed, sitting still,
right in the grassy middle of the track,
I met when I fled up into the hills, that time
my father was dying in a hospital—
I see her suddenly again, borne back
by the morning paper's prize photograph:
two greyhounds tumbling over, absurdly gross,
while the hare shoots off to the left, her bright eye
full not only of speed and fear
but surely in the moment a glad power,

like my father's, running from a lorry-load of soldiers
in nineteen twenty-one, nineteen years old, never
such gladness, he said, cornering in the narrow road
between high hedges, in summer dusk.
                              The hare
like him should never have been coursed,
but, clever, she gets off; another day
she'll fool the stupid dogs, double back
on her own scent, downhill, and choose her time
to spring away out of the frame, all while
the pack is laboring up.
                          The lorry was growling
and he was clever, he saw a house
and risked an open kitchen door. The soldiers
found six people in a country kitchen, one
drying his face, dazed-looking, the towel
half covering his face. The lorry left,
the people let him sleep there, he came out
into a blissful dawn. Should he have chanced that door?
If the sheltering house had been burned down, what good
could all his bright running have done
for those that harbored him?
                          And I should not
have run away, but I went back to the city
next morning, washed in brown bog water, and
I thought about the hare, in her hour of ease.

Ballinascarthy

Is marach an dream úd Caithness dob' ag Gaeil a bhí an lá.
— Pádraig Óg Ó Scolaidhe

There, where the bard Ó Scolaidhe tells the loss
of the great fight when the Croppies met the Caithness
Legion: the date, 1798, cut in brass,

the man driving the forklift truck said: Keep on
straight up the road and you'll see the monument
and turn to your right. But when I had gone

up the long hill to the cross of Kilnagross,
I saw only the spruces that had grown
darkening green on either side of the stone.

After a mile I turned back and drove west, blinded
by dancing flaws in the light, as I passed
under the planted trees, like dashed foam

or the dashes of yellow and white on an old headstone.
Yet in that darkening light I saw the place,
turned left and followed the falling road

for the graveyard. I searched for my great
grandfather's name, Charles Cullinane, but I found
only one Daniel, 1843, one headstone,

and in Kilmalooda I found Timothy's name
on a headstone in the long grass almost lost,
and Jeremiah's, and I found the name *Bence-Jones,*

1971, cut by Séamus Murphy who made my father's stone
in 1970, in the Botanics, and below that another name
in a different hand, Ken Thompson's, I recognized:

Ken Thompson carves the figure 9
in a different style, as in the stone he made
for my mother and her second husband in their Offaly grave.

I left the Bence-Joneses in the long grass
and drove back to the cross
and downhill again past the secret monument

to the dead of the great battle of Kilnagross
where the spruces whistle to each other and the carved stone is lost.

The Door

When the door opened the lively conversation
beyond it paused very briefly and then pushed on;
there were sounds of departure, a railway station,
everyone talking with such hurried animation
the voices could hardly be told apart until one

rang in a sudden silence: "The word *when*, that's where you start"—
then they all shouted *goodbye*, the trains began to tug and slide;
joyfully they called while the railways pulled them apart
and the door discreetly closed and turned from a celestial arch
into merely a door, leaving us cold on the outside.

The Polio Epidemic

No hurry at all in house or garden,
the children were kept from the danger—
the parents suddenly had more time
to watch them, to keep them amused,
to see they had plenty to read.
The city lay empty, infected.
There was no more ice-cream.
The baths were closed all summer.

One day my father allowed me beyond the gate
with a message to pass through a slit in a blank wall;
I promised I would just cycle for two hours,
not stop or talk, and I roamed the long roads
clear through city and suburbs, past new churches,
past ridges of houses where strange children
were kept indoors too, I sliced through miles of air,
free as a plague angel descending
on places the buses went: Commons Road, Friars' Walk.

A Revelation, for Eddie Linden

Ranged, fanned out—as, in the apocalypse of John,
those who were not defiled—the victims,
children, great-aunts, lacemakers and especially
the laborious foreigners, every one
bearing the emblem of his trade:
how quietly they listen to the lines
praising their lives, the voice that trembles
eloquently holding them in place.
The room is upstanding with white pedestals and busts
and a plain, good carpet; there will be coffee soon.
The verses halt and tug. Why do they allow it,
are they bullied or too modest, can they feel honored
by the partial mugshot? Here is the coffee,
and probably whiskey in the far parlor
for the famous who stand and stretch.
                                    And I spot you, Eddie,
stepping back from the spillage,
imprisoned against glass bookcases
where the spines in a row slide from *Assyrian* to *Hittite*
(no script more strange, no dragon a more
outrageous presence than yours) and you draw breath,
because your retreat is partial, and when you speak
a draught from a city of broken windows
will come razoring under the door.

Ascribed

She sat and wrote as if a voice had spoken, *Write*
for those who never made it to the promised shore
who waded ahead carrying what they could manage
above the breast-high flood, the children kicking,
the soft toys saved on their damp shoulders;
how they came to a well-made pillar of stone
built three centuries back after the Williamite wars
locked together out of symmetrical stones
founded on driven piles. And the river spilling
all around it, and the skylarks above a grazing island—

and then the speaking voice was not heard any more, only
the deep gasping of a beast in trouble,
and the voices of the drowned did not reach her at all
but instead it came to her in silence,
an instant: her grandmother remembered in old age
her long hair down, her wide shoulders bare
before her basin in the early light
while the cat lapped a basin of fresh milk,
and how as a child she watched without moving.

Two Poems for Leland Bardwell

I SICILY: CERES AND PERSEPHONE

The ferry slips like chalk
leaving its friable mark, like ice gliding
on a marble counter, its shadow melting in the light,
Catania, where the girls in their circle
in the gymnasium held hands,
embracing, kissing, smiling at me
like a heavenly ceiling, fading.

What seemed at hand (earth
blooming with orange-trees and hotels)
when the train rounded the headland was revealed
in shadow, far away
on the other side of the straits.
I can see through a round hole: water
racing, laughing, and on the dappled ceiling
shadows in backward flight.

2007

II YOU NEVER SAW A BED-END
IN A PROTESTANT FENCE

There is a film of icy dew over
the spread pastures of Leeson Street.
The dandelions fringing the partitions,
the bunched underwear tossed and dangled
across nine-bar gates, are flecked
with frost. The Jesuits
behind walls of transparent mist
move slowly to their prayers, steaming
and solid, like morning cattle.
Below the street the sleepers are herded
horizontal in their sofa beds and horseboxes,
the fuzz of ice on their shoulders,
on their tossed hair, not bothering them
at all; the three children going out to school
whisper and hop between them
in a chink of bus fares.

The area is a breath of cold bright wind
as you climb, holding a child in each hand.
Across the street in 1968
the Garda is still protecting the frozen bus
that carries the strike breakers to the ice factory.
The sun lands on him before anything else in the street.
Every inch of his body is tired
as the melting drops on the railings,
on the telephone wires, on the Georgian weeds,
each one sagging, reflecting the world upside down.

2002

237

Michael and the Angel

for Michael Hartnett

Stop, said the angel. *Stop* doing what you were doing and listen.
Yes, you can taste the stew and add the salt
(have you tried it with a touch of cinnamon?)
but listen to me while you're doing it.
I am not the one who found you
the work in the Telephone Exchange.
That was a different angel.
I am the angel who says *Remember*,
do you remember, the taste of the wood-sorrel leaves
in the ditches on your way to the school? Go on,
remember, how you found them
piercing a lattice of green blades,
and their bitter juice. The grassy roads
that swung in and out of the shade
passing a well or a graveyard,
the gaps and stiles on the chapel path—
their windings, their changes of pace
always escaping the casual watch you kept—
you must go back and look at them again,
and look again the next day, for they change,
there is new growth, or the dew is packed like a blanket.
Later come rose hips and the bloom of sloes,
and you must be there to see them. Your children will find
the sweet drop in the fuchsia flower, swallow it down;
they will run from the summer shower, but your work is to stay,
to hold the pose of the starved pikeman, grasping upright
the borrowed long ladder. After the rain
dries off your shrinking shirt, the blue flower
will shine up from the aftergrass where it nestled.
You will have to guess the size of the steam rising,
how it frees itself, sliding up off the field
at the time when the beeches are dropping their mast,
when the sloes are ripe in the hedge, you might still
find the taste there, among the last of the grain.

The Flood

I'm out again, straying
earnest as ever I quested
in search of the neutral ground—
skirting high fields I look back—
I can still hear the cry.

Did I try this angle before?
The road dips and carries me
out, arched across the Shannon:

not history, not division,
a pure pouring, out of the north.

The midge's glassed patch, the lark's foothold
of raised bog, brims, leaks, tilts,
hithering the trickles merge
in this frosted rush of stasis.

I call on the muscles to shift,
choose, focus, as if I had found
a crack with a spiral glimpse,
and what lies within. But it comes
full against me like a motorway—
I can look nowhere else.

Intense, amplified hiss
of time passing, like nothing...
but singular grief:
repeated, the protest of the mother
by the bed where her daughter lay dead.
The eye can only
relax, distended:
the heart hammering, the danced tangle
of light on the sliding depths.

In His Language

She is breathless, sheltering
in the shallow architect's
groove, the last place you'd expect
an echo of faithful speech—
hearing the voice that taught her
the true note of the wind-harp,
she dashes across, reaches
the wisteria's thick shade
and waits till a sound of hooves
ambles past the rows of peas
to rendezvous with the badger.

The pigeon as big as a dog
explains in his shambling grammar:
all this tuning holds back meaning
while setting it free.
     Remember,
you were the groom that pushed apart
the weight of two standing horses
leaning heavy towards each other
in the darkening stable.

II THE SCORE

Listening to the way that
everything shakes in his language,
the high wind blown through the tenses,
she feels it keen when the tempi
settle faster and stricter—
his house is filled up with sound,
a thick rope wound and fastened
athwart the stairway holds
the walls in place, when the past
rings in the floorboards. And

even upstairs the vibration
penetrates cupboards packed
with volumes of puce-brown paper
stacked flat; if a triplet picked
on a xylophone inquires,
the knotted silk thread stretching
snaring the newel-post frays
with the shiver, a verb twists
to a subjunctive, a cat
rolling over in the sun.

And she ruffles her shoulders:
the cloak she wears, shuddering
opens out, spreads, a carpet
made of the loose-woven stalks
of the Great World-Bindweed,
and every one has a root,
pierces a trickle, and that
bleeds downward: hush, the dangling
strings of glitter hymn the air.

Come Back

Although there is no paper yet, no ink,
there is already the hand
that moves, needing to write
words never shouted from balconies of rock
into the concave hills
to one far away, whose hair
on a collarbone resembles
that break in the dunes, that tufted ridge
he must have passed, faring away.

If the railway does not exist yet, there is, even
now, a nostril to recognize
the smells of fatigue and arrival,
an ear cocked for the slow beginning,
deliberated, of movement, wheels rolling.

If the telephone has not been invented
by anyone, still the woman in the scratchy shirt,
strapped to her bed, on a dark evening,
with rain beginning outside, is sending
impulses that sound and stop and ask
again and again for help, from the one
who is far away, slowly
beginning her day's work,
or, perhaps, from one already in his grave.

The Savage

She opens the stopcock and lets it come bubbling up
filling as far as the reinforced glass floor
and it shines transparent
and is absence that still

laps with its pulsed currents, the muscles
like the salmon pushing; as its fizz settles
she gazes in the deep tank, picks out
the shadows meeting, herself; and the long

quicksilver jaws, and the interlocking lights
pressing summer and the eye into place,
remind her of that swatch
she keeps in her pocket (it packs

every known shade, but when she takes it out
they are all fused into a glowing white—
so the cloud and the sun fuse, the fish and the waterfall)—

so, was it her arm that sliced
half a gown away, the silver

fall, her hand that cut the last line from the letter,
that laid the rooms all open, with their cramped air,
their claw-footed cooking stoves
and their turned-down beds?

Calendar Custom

What is the right name of that small red flower?
It's everywhere, spilling down over the stones
in the sun, every year at just this time.

The color dims for a minute as the line of dust
follows the loud white van uphill, and just now
the girls in the bar offer me a glass of water.

What is that soft smell that is everywhere,
the water reeking like tar? and while the cloud
swells and the rain begins, the man standing

in the yard outside inhales the damp half-hour.
The red is fading again to a pinkish beige;
the plants crouch like cats while it pours down.

The smell is harsher, the light warped panels do
no good, the piecemeal shutters can't keep it out.
Then as his uniform dries to a full blue,

and half of the window brightens, the tall girl throws
the door wide, and the man and the air are allowed
to blunder inside by pillowfulls. She tears

two pages off the calendar. All colors now
bright as a mirror drown out the little flowers
drooping in the soft breeze as their date comes around.

The Clouds

Octaves higher than the peaks, a skirt of vapor
hesitates, a press of cloud permits
globed light escaping, the oriental twirl
I never see without expecting the whinge
of opening gates. The mountains preen their slopes
for invitations, and a high opinionated
forehead in profile, as of a woman
with the face of Achilles and the bare
shoulders of Andromache, gazes—
at which of those barely fashioned heads?—

searches for one who lives in the moving gondola of light
spilled on the chosen earth as the ice slides
off into streams, who lives with people
(for how to do this alone) who are really there,
having names for hunger and thirst, and like them
(how could it be otherwise) can see across the valley
to where on other cliffs the light
paints shapes of heads or trees or gables,
so that one hesitates, takes a step back
for a better view, turning, as when the sun struck,
once, Matthew's counted coins. A new scribal hand
opening (how else does writing work?) arched ways
to see past the hanging nets, see who is there
in the whirling dance, when you duck and catch:
the moment thinning the curtain,
real, like the tricks of the light.

Interim Report to Paul: November

Dusk and a gate, a leaf
turning, a dark place:
the cypress-green endpapers
of a packed book, your filled life.

The ranked evergreens
frogmarch a slim path;
this enclosure, the blocked tombs,
the crosses, repeat, pinning down

their instant of focus,
shuffle the pack, the blades
of darkness, absence. Peace.
And this is where you were taken.

But you are not yet here,
still on the move. The orange
pumpkins you planted are growing in the garden,
the songs you were promised have not all been sung.

Update for Paul Cahill

Here is the place as you knew it—
the pinned lines of agriculture buckling,
pressed up against the dark fringe,
the woods, quilting the secret hills.

The one who walks on the high path looks down:

how long will the worker bend
over the task he knows best,
how long in the ten o'clock heat
will the one seed twirling on its thread
disturb the silence?

The Nave

Learning at last to see, I must begin drawing;
I cast abroad the line
that noses under stones, presses around an instep,
threads off into distance and forward again
as it pierces and drags. Like a daft graph it shoots
up, like a weed falls and rises. I am led, I find it
looped on every hooked corbel. Drowned in deep shadows
I catch myself in a tangle of rickety laneways,
part of a procession. The streets
are full of innocence, a stumbling,
cobbled bazaar of shining bargain treasures,
their shimmer resisting the eye.
Remotely the four-four beat of the carnival march
pulls me aside, adrift on the stepped descent—
a fresh smell from the lemonade stall announces
the square transformed. The trinkets dangle,
ribbons wrap round and round the colored poles.
The air darkens, fairylights burst out on wires;
the line calls me upwards, curving banisters,
their metal studs too nearly worn away,
come to a point where a little troop,
all brightly masked, wait for more companions
before the steeper climb.
                      It is cooler here:
darkish stone, slate, a marble well, a ramp
with a squashed feather stuck to one side, then old,
clean tiles. I am drawn, staggering—
it feels like lifting a tall, swaying ship
with wind-filling streamers—
across the threshold.

And indeed the nave
hums like a ship, the corded masts and spars
are tugged by wind, and the uppermost gallery
swings and revolves. The hanging censer
vibrates like a spider on his thread. In the rigging clings
a saint whose cure is personal as a song
performed aloud at a wake by a special call,
or softly to a patient in her hospital ward.

The Cure

They've kept the servant sitting up;
it's late again,
their fire burning so high they've opened a door,
and from her room

she hears them settling the great questions:
how treat a case
of green-sickness or, again, one of unrequited love?
The fire burns down,

they close the door. She was writing to her mother,
resumes: *Don't think*
of consulting that fraudulent woman. Her sister, who
died, had the gift.

...I understand, it must be hard for her,
so long, no news,
but surely, secretly it comforts her heart
that the child thrives.

The voices boom again, the door is wide,
she hears the bell,
appears with her candlestick, ready to guide
a guest to bed,

then back to her letter. *The lady of this house*
keeps to her room.
The master sighs as he locks the heavy street door.
There is no cure.

The Water

Thin as a wash, does it get any deeper
at all, or could we see its depth, since we catch
only the gleam when the flipped blade
rewards the light, like a silk flash of hair in the water,

and since our eye muscles are slack as the grasp a bare
wall has on the sun painting it white?—

Although like the white of dawn hitting a wall this is real
and the floating shards of light are really there—

and Oh, Hundred-pocketed Time, the big coat lined
with lazy silk pinched close as finger and thumb
various as oceans, precious-tinted like skies,
what upset you to empty them all at once,
what stretched thread long enough to measure the reach,
a lighthouse searching the dark, scraping the sea with its beam?

Vertigo

Shaped like a barrel with asthma, her black skirt
bunched at her waist, she kneels or squats
at every spot reputed to be holy.
Her two daughters wait and gossip until
she scrambles up and they move a few yards on.

How did such smart women acquire such a mother?
She insists on doing the next bit barefoot. "Nobody
does that any more, Mama." But she's down,
one haunch on a pointed stone, handing the shoes
to the younger one, hauling off the black stockings

which she adds to the black bag already encumbered
with rosary beads tangled in keys, all the stuff
she's dragged from home. She struggles ahead,
joining the queue to climb the staggered steps
along the cliff edge. A puffin lands beside her;

she yelps in surprise. Then she reaches out in her turn
to stroke each of five crosses cut in the slab,
one for the saint, four for his four sisters, named
in the early *Life*. (It was here that he overcame
the crooked landlord and set all the tenants free.)

Then off again. The daughters are resigned
to the last sharp ascent. From below, they keep her
in sight. The mainland spreads in the wide distance;
the clouds are scattering, and above them stands
the stony north face of the abbey, the great door—

but photography barely exists. The lighthouse men
have news of the Russian war. The daughters fret,
watching the bumblebees trample the sea pinks
in the spot where last year a man fell and smashed,
how will they ever get her back down to the boat?

She is terrified of heights. The seagulls' diving call,
the foam at the foot of the cliff, make her feel sick,
but she does look down, and at last sees what is there,
the dimensions, the naming. Yes.
A broad slick widening, an anachronism,

ambiguous like a leaf floating where never
a leaf has blown, like a word, a calque, swimming
up into sight through the tides of speech, like a seal
who plays on the deep ocean: the gate of her days left open,
her daughters like armed angels guarding each side
of the path to the edge, where everything pours away.

Where the Pale Flower Flashes and Disappears

Then the waters folded over him
their long leaves their ripple embrace
dissolving the lines of his face
the sky crowded on top of him
the trees held the firmament up in its place
their peacock spread
the last thing meeting his gaze.

The trees began their song the notes
bound to the spot,
a repetitious air turning again
but strong enough
that the stunned mourners found
they were afoot they had walked outside
in the air although
just now they felt themselves sinking
into a grave.

Out of that dark they came and saw the trees—
branches tense like dancers
over their glass—they saw the roots,
a piercing grasp that roved
down, under and between the buried stones.

The Litany

As every new day waking finds its pitch
selecting a fresh angle, so the sun
hangs down its veils, so the old verbs
change their invocation and their mood.

Steady through the long gap in the story
a stiff breeze whistles up off the ocean
choosing a pair of notes, the same key.

A tidal drag sucks back down as deep
as it rode high; the foamy-crested wave
(astonished at numbers, the white gannets,
in their salt generations) arrives
to listen for that same voice and stays,
arching smoothly, waiting for the response.

The soaking tears of centuries drill down
low passages in between the stones,
keeping to the calendar made out

in columns of names, a single stiff skin
coiled up and stowed away in the high slit
above the stone corbel that once had human features.

The wave can pause no longer, called back to Brazil.

In the Mountains

I

You are almost at the end of your journey;
nobody has asked you for help
since the child playing by the yellow gable
who had lost her ball in the gully.
The broad linked chain still weighs down your pocket.

It is early in the mountains,
the mist thronged like blossom,
the grassy road to the harbor
grey with dew, the branches
loaded like a bride with embroidery.

II

Do you remember the dark night
when the voice cried from the yard
asking for water, and you rose from the bed.
You were gone so long, I said to myself at last
As long as I live I will never ask who was there.

But now I want to ask that question.
I see you at the boundary stone and I need
to say the word that will bring her out of the trees:
Notice her: she limps to the field's edge—
a step, a clutch at the baldric, a hand to her hair.

The little stony stream divides forest from field.
She looks away. The wooded scene accentuates
the grace that says *Look—don't look* wavering
like the spring breeze tossing the leaves, her draperies
hesitant, her flexed foot on dappled gravel.

The Sun-fish

Basking shark, An Liamhán Gréine, Cetorhinus maximus

I THE WATCHER

The salmon nets flung wide, their drifted floats
curve, ending below the watcher's downward view
from the high promontory. A fin a fluke
and they are there, the huge sun-fish,
holding still, stenciled in the shallows.

They doze in their long dawdle foraging at edges
where warmer streams collide with cold, westward.
Their matched shadows trail them up the sound.
What secretive ocean hid them since last they surfaced
out of deep *then*? The late bright evening lies
flat on the sea, they press up against the glassy screed
or sink to shades in a delicate layer of smoke.

II OBSERVATIONS AT THE SURFACE

Tracking tides, traipsing,
feeding through their fixed yawn,
they have history, patches,
warm nights with sudden endings.

"The boat was not her measure—
she destroyed the net—
we cut it away and left her
wounded to death."

Others were sighted
passing the Seven Heads
and a year later hundreds
nose-to-tail off the Lizard.

And again: "I rounded the corner
in my father's car. They were there,
exposed, flayed at the quayside,
a bright bloody color exploding,
too big for the quay wall,
too big for the little bay."

III MERE PEDDLING

And again: how fast we forget,
how grimy we see the people: men and women,
the clustered stoves on stony beaches, the various tubs and barrels
rendering the oil from the liver, sediment
settling, useful to curriers, ironfounders
and others. The buyers, the carts waiting;
the voice in each one's head that says *Live, live*;
men able to kill, to impregnate, to hunt
in dangerous boats—"The pale streak over the backbone
is the place to aim the spear: downward"—
able to hack cold carcasses and slave
at the hot iron stoves. And when the sun-fish
had disappeared, to crowd the ships for Ayrshire,
Derby, Cleveland. The women's long cry
the only echo left of all that loss.

IV THEIR SHADOW ON THE SEA

*Krill. Bloom. Copepods. Thermocline.
Elasmobranch. Liamhán Gréine.*

In troops of words they form, a gulp dissolves them.
The ocean swathing the globe is a snake mask.

I watch for the outline, widening the maritime stare.
The angles are a scattered puzzle. I will not

let it take shape yet, trying
to freeze the dappled light and foam.

But they are there already, as the watcher saw them
once, craning as they nosed in under the cliff,

suddenly present, a visitation,
like the faces of my two parents looking at me

from the other side, from the outside
of the misty screen of winter.

In the Desert

Almost day, looking down
from my high tower in the desert:
the sandstorm blows up,
cuts my tower in half:
a crooked scarf of sand
as high as the window
that looks towards the mountains.
I cover my eyes
with my red scarf that slants
wrapping my body
and when it is over
I look towards the desert
and I see him again
in the daybreak light
still walking nearer—
he must be half blinded.

In the desert walking
I see them by the shining,
reflection of dawn light,
something bright sewn in the cloth
worn on the head
masking the face.
I see them glinting.

He is sand brown,
his clothes brown like sand.
Now he is closer
I see his shadow
as the dawn rises,
a bending shadow
and he nears the well
in the shade of the palm trees.

Coming to the well he lifts
its wooden covering. Night
and coolness are still down there.
The snakes lie in the well, males
and females coiled together, wet.
Before he lowers his cup to drink
he salutes them saying, happy
snakes, like the poor people,
who have only the comfort men
and women find in each other.
Let me fill my cup, let me rest
here in the shadow.

I hear him praying, I see him drink.
He lies down in the shadow.

The Cold

The shrine sunk below the level of the traveled road,
reached by smooth, icebound stairs and a cramped door,
holds a single relic in its case of bone.

I have to remember it. Whatever labor, whatever crime
brought me here, I am warned: I am allowed place and time,
not a certificate. I stare and commit, but when I try

to draw, the sacristan (and only now I am aware
he is watching) taps on the glass, points to the notice framed
in five strange alphabets. I search for a known phrase:

only four friendly words open their locks, and those
are stuck like treasures in the grip of grammar, morose,
giving nothing away. Memory, and then Alone,

Memorial, and Creation. I am alone here, I can stay
as long as I please in the cold, printing images in my brain,
I can make rhymes and riddles and rehearse them all day,

around the cracked shapes, the three colors of the stone,
the faces as if through dust returning, the millstone
hitched in its place, the date according to the old

calendar, the capitals with sheaves of corn in relief.
The cold invades my hair and fastens around my ears,
and I catch the echoes of all the shifting minds that here

were braced to carry the same weight. The word that has not been said.
I move out and climb, and the breath of the mountainside
is a new language, and the stream plunging at my side

in the gully under the bridge has its own word
which I could almost understand assuming I could hold
back from inhaling the air of the mountain, and the cold.

The Scrubbing Map

Evening sweeps through the car park, the customers all gone,
when a few old cars arrive with darkness, their tracks
wide, curving past the daytime grid. They end up
collected, all facing inward against the far wall.

The drivers get out, stretch, smoke, then sigh and begin
brushing aside the loose crumple of dirt
mangled after the day, so as to reveal
a wide piazza with angled flights of steps

climbing both sides. They brush the treads
like teeth, clean the risers like a child's ears.
Then moving back across the cleared flagstones,
they change brushes, kneel and begin again—

prestissimo, as if they were polishing glass,
the stone below discloses all its veins,
the bristleworm's shadow chased into the quarried slab,
all the history of weakness charted, the place

where the ground gave in or the lettering wore away,
or the scratched spot where the last one who could read
the frayed relief of graves took a long leave
of the sunk trace. Now they polish again and gaze

through a cloudy floor at the place they left behind,
the deep strait that the ferries face at sunset,
and the shadowy patches, where deeper into the night
a few wrecked boats fearfully make their way.

Like rubbed plans their faces look up out of the stone.
Behind their heads are the maps they will make before dawn
of the way back to their new lodgings,
and where the landlord keeps the spare key, and the butter.

Brother Felix Fabri

The squared interior is tiled
with names, crowded with banners
all bearing devices, twinned
initials, checkered, quartered.

He feels inside his loose sleeve
for the old bone-handled knife
his grand-aunt kept and used
to pare her afternoon apples;

and trims the square of paper—
he has written all the names
for those at home, forgetting
nobody who wanted prayers—

he lays it on the tombstone.
He stands upright, harboring
such clear thoughts about the roads
he traveled he might just fall

asleep. He shivers and picks up
the paper square from under
the crowding feet. And without
stirring at all from his place

he probes the sleeve again, finds
flint and steel, and the heads turn
watching the paper's abrupt
flame, the names that he carried

by all the harsh paths, returned
home in a flourish of ash.

The Married Women

Yes. But you can have no idea
what she was running from,
feared far more than the convent with its high stairs

it was those women with their bangles
their stiff new hats at Easter
their weddings and honeymoons in the Channel Islands.

Their daughters had ponies, the husbands
had business and whiskey. Their hair
was crimped in salons, they met each other for coffee

in town after ten Mass. To the child
they seemed made out of timber and steel,
stiffened by a dose that had penetrated their flesh,

poisoned and tinged them lightly purple.
She avoided them all her life:
then on a Monday morning in a pool dressing-room

she saw a woman, that timber face,
her towel as crisp as ever, her jeans
so stiff and brisk on their hook she thought of the new hats.

The woman turned, and under the towel as if
shrouded by the mantled oxter
of a heroic bird was a girl's mother-of-pearl sheen,

a girl's hesitant body, sheltered by the bird's broad wing.

The Sister

I

How on earth did she manage
that journey on her own?
When she was a young woman
they had plenty to keep them busy,
they were small, they felt queasy,
they gripped a pillar in the shade
and held on,

and as for leaving home—
still, the trains have never changed,
they thunder up the valleys,
built for strapping fellows
flinging their big bundles
easily on to high shelves—
real men.

She turned up at the station,
small, her clothes, once elegant,
all black. Past the train window
slid the suburbs, a fast river.
She saw a white-haired man, waist-deep,
ducking under and rising again—
a cormorant.

II

A lump of a lad handed her bag down to her.
Lopsided she walked as far as the convent door.
They greeted her with a leathery kiss, they told her
where to find her bed and the hour of dinner.

They knew the silent meal would be no surprise,
no more than the hard bread, tougher at every slice,

nor the dead silence of night until the first train
troubled the valley. She would know, lying there,
others were sitting up, working in pairs,
to finish the stitching, tacking the last of the lace.

But the cold woke her, and a subtle mist, as fine
as gauze, hung on the glass. In the freezing dawn
she dragged a web just as light across her skin,
veiling herself for good, and she slept on.

The Liners

All the years she worked at sea the liners
never docked here and, back again on shore,
she watched them anchored at large in the deep water.

She'd sip her tipple of *Stillynight*. The tender swayed,
bumping the steel mountain. The tall steel door
was clamped shut and the ship began the turn,

the yellow portholes glowed, the unloaded tender stood away.
The strung lights brightening curved to the prow, the masthead
a star: the waltzing pyramid enclosing all she knew,

close print of cabins, listed laundry, echoes of command.
It hung like a cloud of midges, like sparks, the bubbles
in her glass. A living face.
                    The wake spread broad
in the twilight, a smooth wave, a mended scar fading
in a sea of idleness, and the moon skating to her door.

Curtain

I laid myself down and slept on the map of Europe,
it creaked and pulled all night and when I rose
in a wide hall to the light of a thundery afternoon
the dreams had bent my body and fused my bones
and a note buzzed over and again and tuned for the night.

We advanced to the window: the square frame showed us
everything, where we had washed up, above rolling domes,
a splash of talk reaching us; behind us we could not hear
how the dark oil-paint slid down the wall
wiping out the way we had come. The measure changed,

the warped foot staggered, I thought
of the yelping music, the interval shaken loose,
I will not hear again. The red-haired bard
rehearsed the bare words that make the verse hang right,
the skewed weights holding in their place like feathers.

The Copious Dark

She used to love the darkness, how it brought
closer the presence of flesh, the white arms and breast
of a stranger in a railway carriage a dim glow—
or the time when the bus drew up at a woodland corner
and a young black man jumped off, and a shade
moved among shades to embrace him under the leaves—

every frame of a lit window, the secrets bared—
books packed warm on a wall—each blank shining blind,
each folded hush of shutters without a glimmer,
even the sucked-sweet tones of neon reflected in rain
in insomniac towns, boulevards where the odd light step
was a man walking alone: they would all be kept,

those promises, for people not yet in sight:
wellsprings she still kept searching for after the night
when every wall turned yellow. Questing she roamed
after the windows she loved, and again they showed
the back rooms of bakeries, the clean engine rooms and all
the floodlit open yards where a van idled by a wall,

a wall as long as life, as long as work.
                              The blighted
shuttered doors in the wall are too many to scan—
as many as the horses in the royal stable, as the lighted
candles in the grand procession? Who can explain
why the wasps are asleep in the dark in their numbered holes
and the lights shine all night in the hospital corridors?

The Boys of Bluehill

An Information

I returned to that narrow street
where I used to stand and listen
to the chat from kitchen or parlor, filtered
through rotten tiles. I thought
the rough walls seemed higher than before.
My cheek against the stone, I noted the new door
since last I'd been there, I began to count the years,

to count the questions I couldn't ask now
(Did you sit apart? Had you washed your hands
before entering the room? Was the water laced
with vinegar? What did you say while it thundered?
And what did you say when you went out
so the crowds that danced at the wedding
would not know your whole story?)

They are dancing still beside the river,
and now I see her climbing towards me
up the long flight of steps that winds
beside the fever hospital,
in her covered basket, the makings
of the meal. I had never
found out the certain day.

And now I must not ask, where did you buy the bread,
and did they guess, in the shop where you got the duck eggs,
that you had a guest? Along the alleys
the wind whispered to me: Open your hand,
let it fall down, whatever you were holding,
let it lie until the day after, let it go,
let it lie until it is blown to the river;

do not look back to see whose hand
finds it, or where it is hidden again when found.

Incipit Hodie

for Phoenix Alexander Woods, born 18 April 2013

When you fell into our language
like a fish into water,
no wonder you were blinded by the splash you made.

We wiped our eyes
but for you it took longer,
it sprayed like feathers around you while you tried

making out the noises. And
slowly the stream ran calmer
though it took you a while to trust your ears and eyes.

How are you supposed
to grasp the water's flow?
But look, those flourishes are pebbles and fish.

Fish are slipping away,
the water is clear and still;
when you reach for words they will be hard like pebbles in your hand.

The Binding

When the train stops at the station he stands up,
moves to the corridor window, looks out and up
at a stone house quite close to the line.

With a stumbling ruin behind it, how it intrigues—
a view suggesting it belongs here,
and yet holds something strange. When I ask,

he says, Yes, I lived there once. I admire
the plain reticent outside. Yes. And do
people live there now? Oh yes, he says,

they have to stay, they have the bindery
and the herd. All that is still going on,
and as long as they stay there nothing will change.

You can see the big press for flattening the books in the shed.
Or at least I can, because I know it is there.

The Skelligs

IN THE STORM

What am I doing here, says the old strong voice,
the wave reaching and snatching
around the pinnacles, faltering and returning
to fling its quilt across the sloping stone
where in the softer days the seal took a rest;
so it wells up, squirting up roses in its fall,
trying again, the awful repeated recoil,
and where is truth under the slamming and roaring,
it wants to know, and *where,*
where is pity now? Gone below,
wiped from the view, and indeed
what has happened to time, as the day's news
is repeated, bellowing like the storm?

TRACKING THE PUFFINS
IN FLIGHT FROM CANADA

No, not yet dawn. A shifting
intensity of dark. A deserted room. Inside,
screens take dictation from satellites. They twitch,

they go still. The storm-beaten flock
signals again, a scattered fistful, drifting.

Labeled like seeds by species, their losses slide
into statistics.
             The gale of wind
they are crossing blows still fiercer
up the Beaufort scale.
                 Then they fade away

…for now. Some day we will count their soft squeaks
in burrows, their whispers to the little fish, blind
under sand. Not yet,
              though here it is clear day.

OUTDOORS

In summer the rain falls slowly at the junction,
the bushes have grown, hiding the station sign,
the holly tree we knew so well is taller
so the clock on the town-hall tower no longer tells us the time—

Nobody thinks we'll go on our travels again:
hunger and cold and carrying loads are all
far away, the wind and the birds' famished complaint,
far as the moving tanker on the grey horizon,
                                        as hardly gained;
until the morning when the mist rises at six,
the shadows lie flat, a thrush on a branch speaks his mind,
somewhere a boat swings away from the stone steps,
an engine kicks and stammers again until it fires.

Somewhere Called Goose Bay

Just looking at the map in the long cold corridor
before the door opens for breakfast, I can see
how countries are nibbled out of continents,
their edges footholds to scramble ashore,
how they bite a coastline, give a name to a harbor—
something flew up reminding one of his home—
or an inland name—*Omaha beach*! Or
calling a whole stretch *Le Côte d'Ivoire*.

Long tables in the refectory, a scrambled icon
where a third hand surfacing on a Madonna breast
seizes a leg askew, its prehistoric sandal
intruding like a memory in the silver plating—but how
to cope at all with the past, since to my own mind
I appear to have been born in 1870
and schooled in 1689? I am stranded
in the pilgrim hostel where the only advice
I have been given is not to comment
on the goat's hair in the butter, if indeed
it is fair to call it butter. Presently
a spruce old woman—I have seen her photograph—
is to come and inform me about the last four
millennia. We will work at a clean corner
of the high table. I will drag her a chair.
For the moment there is nobody here except me
and the man who stands by the door. I've asked him
why it should be goose, he said what is a goose?
He says, *Eat it up. You've surely paid for it.*

From Up Here

The forest floats over the land,
the island slides across the sea;
they appear less firm than the shadow
cast by the plume of steam
voluminous over the power station:

nothing stable except for the gleam:
a flame distilled, neat
as the glare of the lighthouse, pointing,
speaking directly as the sun
to the eye it beckons, its brief

slanted tale of deep distance
surfacing for the instant: this
is real, it says, like
the hours of your past,
those roots with their population
of slugs and slaters.

Indoors

Look in the iced-up glass:
can you read the shadowy blotches?
Are those fish, skeletal boats
learning low tide?

The alabaster lamp reflects
almost the whole dark day, measuring
light on the veined stone fireplace,
its curdled white and grey

the map of a language
spilling across a border
words retreating back in the throat,
the tight mountainous enclave,

as in the five days she lay without a word,
five glasses of milk huddled on a shelf,
congealed, the sun of a winter afternoon
breaking through curtains, piercing the shining whey.

Fainfall

It's dawn, she opens the door to the yard.
Twilight is framed. A pillow of fog.
No sign of the cat. She stands there, inhaling fog;
this is the time when she is almost at ease.

Something stirs, a binding slipped
gently slides down. Is she alone
in her house? A rustling answer
clears away to silence, which lasts and lasts.

With the door wide open, still hesitating,
this is the moment when for once she feels at ease.

I Used to Think

I used to think I needed to sleep—
it sucked me down
in long dreams of daybreak.
I used to say, do what you know
how to do. I do,
nervously I enter the ruined priory,
I greet the bats and pigeons,
I fall asleep,

and at once
roaming again backstage,
a new step feels higher than the old one,
the dressing-room door's rehung,
but the old tune played on the keypad
freezes in memory, locked
in the moment I wrote it there—

The knitted shawl dumped when the moths riddled it,
gone, the car scrapped long since,
discs and logbook, squashed in the wakeful mill
that once consumed the house keys years ago
saved from Córdoba: the tunes, though,
The Boys of Bluehill, Miss Canty's Reel,
the orchestral variations
with the lewd words added to the symphonies,
will follow me when I wake, if I ever wake again.

Who Were Those Travelers

Out there at the edge of the stubble field
slipping past, in pairs or singly, their gait
betrays them, the cloistered shuffle:

an old recognition, like fear
persisting as the lost path winding
in shade refuses, regains

its rutted dust each third summer.
Something has intervened, they are not
elemental as before, exile has changed them;

they are thin as air, as a leaf that has stayed
a century inside a book. They slip like knives
behind the arcades of thistle, on their way

to the emptied shrine. Only the soldiers
in their chopper can see where the grass changes color
over the foundations. They take aim, and

the moving figures fade from the earth one by one.

Stabat Mater

At last the page is peeled away,
the last page, like a covering from a wound,
and the transparent sheet beneath is another page
on which is written, *"You have no enemy."*
—Just look. It is damage itself, and what lights up
the scarred flesh to the view
of the flinching eye, of the one
who saw it all and let us know, in words
we can't read rightly, until touch teaches—

as you can only find out by pushing
forward in the crowd
until your body is pressed
flat against the glass.
Behind the glass is the shadow of suffering,
and it shivers because it feels your touch,
it's alive. But others are pressing
behind, and you must move along,
and when you look back
to the house of mourning
the shutters inside shutters have closed
down, folded, each one with a day's date.

When the calendar was in its force
they all fitted together
as the leaves fit the tree
of atrocities, and even now
you can still hear the elation
of the strings, their long hopping
as the alto fills her lungs
to lead off *Stabat Mater.*

A Musicians' Gallery

It echoes with tapping, chatter, jabber,
noise converging on a teased-out sound;
harmony remembers and at last
squeezes into a dominant, as the angel
tests the note he has found
in the depths of the lute, wringing
resonance from a tight string.

His body freezes alert, as a voice
echoes around the stars. The saint
beside him seems at once listening and singing.
He listens
         (and two rooms away
a man listens to his son
who is tensed around air, breathing
a stave that flutters and blows away—

to land at a wedding, where pipers clutch
bagpipes awkward as bulging animals
kicking to escape the clamped elbows.
The dancers hammer the floor; no rest this night;
the wedded pair sit steady. At another wedding,
the flute player on a cramped balcony dangles a leg
over the rail, still playing.)
         Who is listening,

who can catch the lost bar? The f-shaped hole
on the cubist violin swallows it up until
the fiddler's return to haul it out, bend
her shoulders in a crouch, alert for the signal
to release the note again, matching
the wedding racket and the heavenly echo
calling to the angel to let his own note sound.

It is not natural for an angel,
but he must do it, the long note pushing him
into a body. Now the feet first learn
the push, the calf muscle stretching, the heel
groping for purchase to fit the vibrating ground.
This is where he finds presence, the tug and pressure,
flesh holding the music in place, company.

The Burden of Cloth

The one playing the Cardinal is attended
by troops of acolytes to carry the loaded train.
The light pauses on the fine wristbands,
on the stem glass held high, the tight lip,
the sip and sniff that condemns. The director
calls time, everyone struggles out of the skirts—

and still it's not clear which one is the star player.
They've gone, and the clothes are abandoned in piles:
the nuns' veiling, the calico painted with wild scenes,
the lace all full of holes. The studio curtains
are lined and patched at random to stifle sound,
but a window falls open somewhere and down they come tumbling.

There like the ranged cumuli they must wait looming
until someone comes to carry them all away.
—So who can it be, and is it because of the colors,
ghosts of burgundy, pale roses, that misted white,
that he stands there, shuddering like a flame wedded
to its candle, guarding a greyness at its core, waiting,

which is why it seems so difficult at last to handle and stack
the whole folded history balanced on two bone shoulders.

Here

A note on the table. Your aunt will be here
soon. He spends an hour in the wrong chair reading
her colored magazines under a red rug.

His mother is coming here. Soon—when she finishes
talking to the nurses. The house is clean and bare,
a knife clangs on the stove, his aunt has decided

she'd better feed him. The long room upstairs
he will sleep in tonight is empty, a space
grief has hollowed. His own place, a home hollowed

to fit him, as a bird in its equal nest,
as a tortoise encased in its tortoise shell,
expelled him into ordinary time

which is a long time, and travels a long way
to bring him to the edge, from where, looking back,
he can see the chair, and the red rug, the colored

covers of the magazines, and everything that followed.

The Orchestra Again

As in the story, a helmet floating
                              half sunk in the mountain pool
where the rough stream falls ·
                              and pushes the dead leaves
flapping at the brink,
                              a mouthful of cold water
from a rusty cup.
                              Could that have been his, she wondered.

The bell of brass on the stones.

II

An echo rouses the bright brass chords
when the wind section veers about and then
goes skittering downstairs, until
the strings respond, forging boldly uphill—

Is that you? I have lived another twenty-odd years
with the kettledrum knocking, the chuckle
of the woodblock like water over stones
that taste of brass in my mouth, waiting—

I have lived as all do now, in a fragile, woven
tower of sound that pauses sometimes
until the first violins enter together, they climb
the tower stairs and they climb again, then,

at last, silence. I wait for the voice
that tells me if it's your bow arm that I heard,
your scored fingers that played, lost
in the ensemble, playing to lose, or better

pianissimo, to be lost in the diminishing sound.

The Knot

When the house is dark and the air
quiet for a minute,
then past the window flits
that winging shape like a burning bird
that shoots back on its track and away
again, springing.

        The evening fire
crackles now, the flame slips along the kindling,
the baby flames begin to grasp, they bravely reach,
while the air outside is as clear as water,
and the flying thing is here again, it comes back as if
to a knot that will not loosen, or the small
disturbance in the stream that reveals the snag,

back to that knot whispering in water that shuddered
past my knee, a clutching—
little waves like double quotes—

when the surface of the water glittered like a Christmas tree
and after twenty-one years the hanging glass butterfly
that I bought in the December market slithered away,
lost itself, loosed the knot and fell into its freedom.

Direction

Searching about again to find my father
I must take a step backwards, for in the time
since last I saw him he has moved and changed
more than in all of his life—

he is a mountain becoming a mountain range,
a sliding dance of peaks, their names picked from his list:
the words remembered from the internment camp
that gave him his phobia of candles, his cardplaying codes,
the pipe he never smoked with its ivory bowl.

As he believed that foreign words were real,
their declension revealing even what crawled away
refusing to be learned—in that belief

so many troubles he shed, he leaves
me what I would leave behind for you:

they need not last forever;
they need not lay you forever low.

Anne Street

I still find the matches holding her place
in Gay's *Fables*, or Hobbes. The spines have suffered.
Those days, she worked at a desk on the landing, slept
on a sofa, her glass at hand. She cooked from expensive tins
in a stairwell kitchen. The strutting pigeons nested
against the chimney, where her chair caught the balcony sun.
John slept in the orderly bedroom. Who gave them
a gallon of twenty-year-old Jameson as a wedding present?
She met a man in the alley exposing his private parts
(which she told me were not at all undersized) and tried
persuading him to join her, and meet her friend the psychiatrist
in the corner lounge. That was kind. Now I would ask her
what had happened, that she was in such disarray, as one
might search for a defense. But she had done no wrong.

Juliette Ryan and the Cement Mixer

The world is beauty and order,
beauty that springs from order,
but more, it is a breathing surface a rippling
a fragrance like spice enticing from the kitchen—
a pulse beating behind the embroidered veil,
a branch spreading leaves against sky,
displayed like hair on a pillow,

a pulse like the one that lay beneath
a heaving, shining grey sludge of concrete in the mixer
as the blades revolved inside,
so that she reached out her hand
as if to touch.
        But her brother grabbed
her elbow in case she did touch and finished
losing the hand.
        I want like her to touch,

as if reaching out to lay my hand on velvet
or on the skin of a muscular chest
             or as Byron,
after traveling through four cantos, and eight years,
through four hundred and ninety-five Spenserian stanzas,
and across Europe and Turkey, so at last
he could finish with that pilgrim Harold and meet himself
as a child,
      said
that he laid his hand on the mane of the dark blue sea.

Youth

I might go back to the place
where I was young. This wide terminal city—
and I've lived so much longer here—
fills up with corners; I turn,
all I have done combines to excavate
a channeled maze where I am escaping home.

When I had to walk past the old house
on the way to the hospital I looked
straight ahead, I spent the day
avoiding the windows, while
wheels unwound the corridors.
Going home past the philanthropic flats
I saw where the baked red frieze unwinds
the date in flourished numbers,
a cloak of soot sealing it—
it does not want to be looked at:
the floating curls melt away; the flowing hands
curve, do not grasp, not quite;
                              the paid line

almost lost quivers, there still,
as a child going off down a hill
turns at the curve of a crescent,
dissolving in light, in the view
from where her aunt sits marking her piebald
galleys on her porch: turns again, and shouts goodbye.

Judgment Day

For once, here's a subject where no corner is left
for a cat or a lion, there's no shelf
for a parked cardinal's hat, no neat
stack of wood for winter, no tools
tidy on their hooks.
                  Nobody calmly
pouring wine or hoisting a weighty barrel,
not even a window or a door to admit
light from a garden or a bare yard—
only rising bodies and falling, and odd blown scraps,
or bolts unrolling, of colored cloths,
wide falls or skimped ends.

Is this where they were bound, the robed
processions of my childhood that wound past
open doors with hallstands, area gates,
narrow entries, wisely departing cats?
Away from every angle, every weight
sinking into our lives like the mark
of a body in a bed? To this great quarrel where
nothing is real, only the teeth and the bite
and the cascading remnants
that curtain away all that has passed?

The Signorelli Moment

She's back. Key in the door,
Dr. Proteus feels giddy. Was this the house?
Didn't she remember
a frescoed wall with resurrected limbs?
There's a thump of a hoover, a radio plays,
a dead person greets her.

She's dead too, she thinks. A smooth nude
salutes a skeleton and gestures to introduce
while another levers
a strong thigh bone out of white clinging clay.
Flesh has fallen away.
Politeness covers,

Dr. Proteus considers. She looks around
for the service entrance, and finds
back yard, rubbish bins,
a fire escape. She climbs, inhales,
but something grips her by the ankle,
means business.

Finding Proteus

Queen Méabh standing on the top of Tulsk
could see her way as far as the plain of Louth
at the start of her great raid. Harder to get back home
as the traveler found, harder to look back,
still harder to answer them, those cries from far away,
from the rock in the salty gulf, where nobody
hears them, but they yowl as loud as Judas.

I searched for Dr. Proteus, I found her but
Oh, don't ask me for it now, I'm killed
with the lot of you, says the voice climbing—
she's spotted a crotch in the rocks where she could maybe
see further again. If she'd give me a chance
I might be able to guess the beginning, and how
everything arranges around it, my history,
and the bits that don't belong. Up there,
Dr. Proteus hanging holds the perspective glass—
but how through all her changes and her daft
excuses, how to tear it from her hand?

For Eamonn O'Doherty, 1939–2011

after Ileana Mălăncioiu

It must have been quite a blast if it sliced
the side off that house. The rooms
are all open, tilted, their T-squared angles
preserved, the bits and pieces all astray,
and a tall powdery cloud rises.

The shock has blown old bills and laundry
across the floor, piled like leaves;
the dog's toys have fetched up in the sink,
while the old suits in the upstairs lobby
creak, askew but still on their hooks.

Pictures swing and find a level so
their conversations can continue,
still quite aware that in each room
is a piece of a vast shadow, and
even his shadow is hairy, has teeth and warmth.

In one frame a crimson sunset is obscured
by a branch with crimson apples; and now
an apple falls and rolls, fetches up at the root of the tree.
The shadowed hand reaches, there's the sound of a bite:
they still belong to him, they still have the taste of apples.

The Distance

for Maighréad Uí Mhurchú

Even with her beside him in the boat
he never liked the water, he fingered a stone in his pocket;
but she looked back at the town of Youghal
where she grew up, she saw the pleated wake
and the long lines delighted her, their fading distance
where a line of waves hemmed an edging of sand,
a line of houses crouching, and between

the boat and the land swam a vacant pool of light—
and beyond that absence lay a world, that was sold
for huddling doubts and envies. She would see
across the pub lounge where the ladies ordered brandies
the discretion of light, the indigo tones
of their new suits for Easter, warm as a plum;
she would feel the gap she could not cross again.

*

When she drew a line on the floor with chalk
and I stood behind it, I could see
how firmly shapes were herded, how they clung:
the stones of the graveyard nudging the steeple,
the roof of a shop pressed down by the barracks wall,
and where the stone steps crossed the railway line
a dark tunneled space opening like memory.

Across that pause, remember her. The crime novels,
the cigarettes, the bottle of stout, her back kitchen
kept cold by the damp cliff behind it, so the milk
stayed fresh. *The old tree whispers its news
to the trailing bramble, the roots of the whitethorn finger
the founding stones under the ring-fort, whose shape
can best be seen in the distance, dark against the sky.*

Two Poems for Pearse Hutchinson

A CONVERSATION

"My thoughts are all a case of knives."
— George Herbert

Although the library is like a case of blades,
every one sharpened and the sharpest closest to hand,
and although the floorboards are piled high, the volumes
a stair, sometimes a cascade, a weir with fish traps—

because there was only one player of this game
played on a scaffolding that sprang up, equipped
with snakes and ladders and slides, planted
with oubliettes and excursions that led to chambers
open as in dreams on velvet corridors
lined with colors as strong as ink—the thread
guiding us shone deviant as it plunged
under shadows and surfaced, then lapsed
as a looped line on paper (the frame
comes into focus again, we are back with the shelved
and stacked books to prompt us)—but
there was only one reader, and this time
he has not waited to explain
the rules of the game, which will not be played again.

SMALL

A word you were inclined to: "a small plant,"
"a small, old naked man";
never used in a negative sense:
the small difference intrigued you,
between a word in Catalan and its Castilian cousin;
the dense closeness, the narrow gap
distancing the genitive plural in Irish
from the nominative singular,
the narrow vastness between a broad and slender *r*:
fear, fir,
like a small woman reaching up
to stroke a tall man's muscled shoulder,
as in
To Maria Spiridonovna on Her Keeping
a small gift: eggs and cherries, in Moscow in 1920—

and in Moscow six weeks after you died, as the metro stations
filled up with soldiers on the day before the election,
I imagined messages maybe flying home
in the small languages, in Welsh, Galician, Platt-Deutsch.
I tapped one out: "Saighdiúirí i ngach áit.
Ní rabhadar ann ar maidin." It bounced back.
I could see the small languages clustering
like swallows on wires but then caught like the birds
beating their wings madly against the mad cage
of the imperial tongue. I watched a woman soldier
helping a small old grandmother on to the train
beneath Stalin's huge high arches at Mayakovskaya.

Witness

Why doesn't she speak when they ask her
what has happened? Or she could point
to the film, to the arrested
frames showing a man
bent, carrying something
far too high and various,
too loosely stacked, his life;
and the next frame showing
how he crosses the darkened surface
of the river in flood, how
on the slimy footbridge he's caught
by the gusting wind, how parts
of the load begin to slide.
The sequence ends before
showing him as he stands
holding the last piece
in both hands, so we never
see the face, the camera
never close enough to explain.

The light when she remembered
after the storm had passed
was clear as a day in Galway
when the rain stops, when the sun
shines wide on bog and lakes;
it fills her now with light
until she can't hold any more,
until her tongue cannot move.

The Sentence

Go home and sleep, sleep for ten years if you can.
Fight your way through the dreams, no doubt they will come
hoisting their scenery, the half-painted flats that suggest
scruffy hotels, the dull coarsely padded walls
of crowded bedchambers, cramped stairwells,
where you will spend hours in odd company,
where the dead are awkwardly present, and the estranged
are close but do not explain their savage letters,
while the child you forgot to fetch from school
goes alone on dark bus journeys along the boulevards;

If you wake at last on that other day, on the far side of the dream,
and find the trees have grown, the grass is ripe as hay,
and the old envelopes burned with the other rubbish,
if no crouching orphan waits by your door,
you are free, though not to forget, you can bless the summer,
though you will hardly know yet how many summer seasons
you passed in those inner chambers under the ground.

Teaching Daily in the Temple

Hosea, 6:6

The crowd in its bunches, men near me,
some women hunkered low on the ground,
a child at the breast, one girl standing tense
as an archer focusing—why should I recall them all
(and even a thin man distracted looking away)
and still I can't recover the moment just
when he took and opened the book and began
reading?
        or so I gathered

by the way their attention changed.
I heard, *If you knew what the words meant
in the prophecy of Hosea.* Then the noise
of readying the sacrifice began. I was there,
and so was the column of the Court of Women
solid between him and me. The offerings flowed
into the treasury beside the chair, where
he opened the book.

If you knew what this means.
They were angry then and picked up stones to throw,
and he hid away from them, so that day he escaped.
In my memory there is an interlocking,
a clutch of enclosures fitted together: the burnt
offerings, the altar of incense, the loaves
of proposition on the table for the priests,
gates and thresholds as pure

as water washes.
The wall of the inner court was tall and blank:
a clean place, nothing growing, the water
from the spring and the cisterns running off
with the blood of sacrifice. The colored veil
ruffled in the breeze. And in among them,

between those barriers, the book now closed
and the phrase I missed
still there in the coded
labyrinth I must infiltrate again,
the language of the scroll construe, hunt down
between those hedges an escaping prey
before night falls on the phrase, on the lips
that move in the grave.

Mosaic of the Emperor's Dream

Found is how they feel, herded in his dream of sheep
crowded around him, warm but not quite taking shape,
crushed between bed, book and lamp; and then the walls appear,
the tall gates, and more sheep that push into the town.
The hidden voice that calls them is his own.

They keep coming, their breath steams in tight alleyways.
Raddled on their wool are their archangelic names,
a high grid of orders shining as bright as flame—
they are so many, but known each one by its name—
he is shepherd and ruler with an imperial frown.

They are so many, they move forward like the waves
breaking over the quilt and the pillowcase
as the sea rises and the gates crash and fall down.
Says the voice: You called us as sheep, but as angels we came,
and one of us is the swordbearing angel that will break apart your town.

Dieppe, 1956

Fresh, I remember, like bleached cloth, like lemons,
fresh as the ribbons and cherries
printing my white cotton dress:
whiteness of ivory in the auction room—
an ivory gentleman, whose feathered hat, curled wig,
his boots and spurs, all shone smooth white,
wore a hinged coat. It opened to reveal
"a triptych adorned with scenes of battle"

                                                because
before the slave trade reached its height, it was ivory
they carried in ships (like that one, with ivory sliced
for sails, with hawsers fine as linen threads)
plying the Atlantic coast, so the workshops thrilled,
working the white teeth into that fine mock lace
to frame a miniature group of Calvary.

The Incidental Human Figures

A bunch of rascals playing with dice
in this print of Piranesi's are at home
on the steps of an ancient temple. The fisherman
is at home on the river bank and doesn't see
the man behind him walking with a dog. The shepherd,
his long staff the only vertical line
winding along in the foreground of the etching
of the ruined abbey, trails Biblical sheep—
whose tinkling bells you cannot hear. They all say,
This is peace, those ruinous days are gone,
the humble, ignorant, even the idle
can live safely now; these do not care
about monks or goddesses, they are small,
and over their shoulders towers the ruinous past.

What about the sailor
whose fragile craft is tossed about in the oil painting
under some famous cliffs? He has been summoned
to show the scale, to suggest the grand force,
proportion, disproportion. What grand consent
invades his heart as the sublime
soaks him, and swallows him down?

Even Then

Even in those days it has to have been the same,
in the first cities of all,
lights showing, early houses, guards breaking their fast,
a pale woman serving them,
birds arguing with cats or beggars. Then the insomniac's
long-desired consolation:
the accents of people in from the country with goods
for market.
            City workers
leave worrying lives behind for tasks that have names
and limits, or put on shoes
to clean after somebody's nightmare. She can sleep
till noon, while early risers
drink up the air of dawn, while time is shuffled;
in some room the musicians
are testing echoes; just then the card game begins again;
and elsewhere the grandmother sits in shadow,
very slowly shelling peas.

Dream Shine

When I switch off the light
the darkness lasts only
an instant, they appear

like women in their doorways
hesitant, brandishing
their dim lamp. The shine

reflected from deep snow
edges the darkness
of a hanging gown,

singles out a surface,
a beam sliding upwards,
a gleam suspended;

a slice wriggles up
from a fountain in the courtyard,
slips into the room,

finds itself a shelf,
bobs beside it—
who would not prefer

to sleep surrounded
by these gentle intruders,
wrapped in their whispers:

*Go to sleep, dream about
the mouse that used to watch you,
looking out from his door*

*in the dashboard, sidelong,
as soon as the engine growled
and the car moved on its road?*

The Gift

A hand rooted in a pocket—
of leather and old fur, it seemed—
jingled all the syllables till,
offering the gift, reaching out,
it slackened its hold:
            the girl's hand
stretched and grasped, kept the gift safely,
walking, all three days and three nights
along dry paths, past closed houses,
fields of thistles and empty barns.

It was enfolded, covered, tucked
neatly away in its Latin,
clasp and hasp severe and entire,
the beasts embracing, their jaws clenched,
the human-headed manticore
        and the jealous angels watching.

She kept them from tearing her, nights
repeating rhymes of ablatives,
prepositions.
        She saw a gate
before her: there was work and food
and a place to sleep. She waited,
still, for the urgent moment when
she would open the clasp, the day
when the deadlines could all go hang
while for hours till dark she handled
pages, reading the words out loud.

The Skirt

The young girl standing
at the head of the long staircase
with her long full skirt
of black lace embroidery
holds her precious fiddle,
her long slim bow in her right hand.

She has never, nobody alive
in this town has ever seen
a woman descending stairs
with such a fullness of cloth
managed, or knows how it's done.
Her grandfather sighs, puts aside his graveclothes,

the spectacles, crossword, pencil,
to show her how his mother,
his grandmother, dressed a stairway—
how one skilled hand rightly placed
on the flowing, trailing herd
jerked all smoothly into a parade.

She starts to make her way
down and the risers behind her
all flower in shiny blackness,
glitter in gaps of lace
following her down along;
and when she reaches the floor it opens.

She treads on down, the stairwell plunges away,
her feet still find the trail, she still holds the fiddle
upright, the white flash of the bow fading.

Passing Palmers Green Station

The train flies through the station; and here is where
for years I would step down to the platform
and climb up the long stairway to the road.
On it goes, past that other station,
where my mother lost one shoe in the gap, coming back
from the hospital where she'd left her younger daughter
among the dying. My weight on the same ground,
the rails and the overhead wires the same,
the labors of the bones. The train dips
under the ground, and for the last stage
of this journey I am close to them, to the gap
that resembles the dark side of the moon in Ariosto,
where Astolfo flew on the hippogriff, and discovered
that everything lost on the earth can again be found.

The Percussion Version

Music is why we live inside
these foursquare rooms, why we gather
to listen to the scrabbling and the sound test,
the way the splash cymbal explores the limits,
vibrating against the glass, and the bell note
rings and rises like a cloud into the ceiling.

From outside the house how different: I paused
beside the door and all I could hear
was a chair scraping into silence
and presently a soft step climbing,

a sigh from the upper floor, at which
in the room below something knocked just once
and the well in the back yard answered
with a bass vibrating groan.

The Words Collide

The scribe objects. You can't put it like that,
I can't write that. But the client
is a tough small woman forty years old.
She insists. She needs her letter
to open out full of pleated revolving silk
and the soft lobes of her ears
where she flaunts those thin silver wires.

She wants to tell her dream to the only one
who will get the drift. How she saw their children lying,
every one dressed out in their simple fears. They glowed,
the shape of their sentence outlined in sea green.
Among those beloved exiles
one sighed happy, as a curtain
lightened and the grammar changed, and the wall
showed pure white in the shape of a bird's wing.

But when she whispered it to the scribe he frowned
and she saw she had got it wrong, she had come
to a place where they all spoke the one language:
it rose up before her like a quay wall
draped in sable weeds. He said,
You can't put those words into your letter.
It will weigh too heavy, it will cost too much,
it will break the strap of the postman's bag,
it will crack his collarbone. The bridges
are all so bad now, with that weight to shift
he's bound to stumble. He'll never make it alive.

The Mother House

An Imperfect Enclosure

for Nano Nagle (1718–1784)

She was out in all weathers.
She was tired, someone gave her
a chair in a shop. Rested
and then away, in the street, on the move.

The house she built first, giving
on the street—could she close up
doors and windows on that side?
It would be noticed as a convent.

She asked to be buried in
the common cemetery.
They broke through the wall
of the nuns' graveyard

and slipped her coffin inside.
But she would not stay,
so they built her a stone tomb
nearer to Cove Lane

and opened a latch at one end
so hands can touch the coffin.

She Was at the Haymaking

She was down in the small field
turning the last swaths of hay
on the slope facing the river mouth

(each time she came back up
she saw the wave so gently courting
the land with shallow pushes

and the curved edge of the tide
making its way upstream)
she was alone in the field—

they were up in the house with Mary
whose bag was packed, waiting for the car
to bring her on the first stage,

the start of her long voyage
away to the far shores
of America and the novitiate.

She worked on with the rake
thinking of the rolling wave,
an eye watching for the car.

When she heard it on the road
she brought the rake up with her
on the steep path to the house.

They were all there in the parlor,
Mary sitting in the middle,
her face amazed. "I can't go.

"Now that it's time, I can't go."
Her parents said nothing. Her sister
had come to bid her goodbye,

now she said, "So I'll go."
She shook a small bit of hay
out of her hair. She washed her hands,

she took up the bag and went off with the driver
to a house full of rules—so far away
that when she wrote to say she was happy

the letter took three weeks crossing the sea.

A Journey

I went driving through the countries
where I could read the names,
the posters outside cinemas,
the leaflets in the churches;

the scripts began to slow me down
after the mountain border climb
and beyond the roadblock I could see
only the shapes: the shed end

and the parked van, and the slow-
motion shadow of somebody
at the edge of the road. I looked
again at the deep wound in my arm;

it was all cleaned and covered up,
so as not to frighten the children.

The Unreconcile

The numbers work their tricks, dividing and stacking in columns
that shake when a draught from an open diary or
an old account-book slips its blade in between:
nineteen-sixty-seven, seventy, seventy-one, seventy-eight,

eighty-three, eighty-four, eighty-nine, two-thousand-and-nine.
A boy fretting on the bus to school is one.
A girl on the train from Fishguard to Oxford is one.
A woman in London queueing in Outpatients is still one.

Exile-sex-death: just as Charles Baudelaire saw the swan
on the building site in Paris, grey webbed feet on the dry
stones, his open beak, stretched neck, in the pose Ovid
explains is peculiar to human beings, and he thought

about Andromache's tears, the little river she invented,
about the consumptive African woman tramping the foggy street,
he thought of slender orphans withering like flowers,
of the defeated, of stranded sailors, and so on—

nothing can shift the weight, the hundred stones in the school yard
are founded on deeper buried stones, a hundred
men and women are crying in underground hospital car parks—
no river and no rain can wash any of this away.

Love

The view from the train is better than a dream.
A man is gazing down his lines of beetroot,
a lone tractor waits at the level crossing,
one light glowing although it's not quite dark.
A doll has fallen into the gloom of the hedge,
her frilly skirt still white. Walls come closer,
lights on Clara station cast their orange trawl.
Beyond its margin the engines
vibrate in the carpark, harmonizing the hum of love.

A newspaper spread on a dashboard
catches the last light from an office window;
a parent's overcoated shape is reading,
waiting for the noisy gang that clings
by the doors with their luggage while
the wheels are slowing and finally slide and stand.

Kilmainham

Tell me he said how you managed to break out of my jail
so that I can build a better one that will not fail.

So I explained about the whistle and the gin,
the special shoes and so forth, and I threw in

the ropes made out of blankets, the false handcuffs, the vitriol,
the cunning tailored loose-cut trousers, the tobacco-pipe, and all

to distract him from the innocent who passed down the high wall
at my side, who is wandering the world now
transparent as the ocean, direct as the shallow flow
of tides over stones, will he make it home, or must he fall?

On the Move

Arthur Maximilian Woods, August 2015

The path turns right, and turns again where the sheep
spotted a sweeter tuft of grass—
it halts by bridges, under trees, it keeps going—
Arthur is ready to follow, he stands
barefoot on the cool grass. Go on, Arthur,
follow the path, walk on the grass not the gravel, until
when you look back the house has disappeared.

The window seems quite plain while he is out of view
and when he surfaces again our sight
fills up like a full glass. It's the trick of a road
emptying itself, a stage where someone's
hidden by flat forest scenery, and when the cue arrives
he passes along remote and small
until turning to meet us again, making for home—

loaded, we'll see, when he empties his pockets,
with mountains, friends, pine cones, clouds and such stuff.

Resemblances

My mother nodding down at me from her portrait
in the hall never looked so still in her lifetime,
only when she sat for Edward McGuire
who loaded her with a black cloak from Kinsale.
She does look like herself though,
as Adam looked like God
but also looked like Eve.
Do I look like her? I am older now
than her age when she died.

I head upstairs and see myself,
and see my room, the books
on their shelves, all the wrong way round,
rearranged in the beveled glass of my aunt's
complicated sideboard which sits
across the landing from the study door.
Like everything that I deal with now the room
has a double, a frill of light surrounding it.

When I kill the landing light
the books are still present for a moment
in the glow from the laptop screen facing the shelves,
their new regime still briefly stamped
in the memory of mercury and glass.

The Blind

One broken slat pulled from the blind
shows only a slice: the marbled clouds,
a world of bright sky stretching.

But she can't look out. The news,
a thread that crawls and winds, drags her
into the dark well

that widens then pulls tighter:
what is down there is heavy
and it is true. It pulls on her skin.

All of her is in here,
it is all in the rule, every stitch that
she is wearing, every minute

in the table of the day, each
close-packed piece of type
that printed her instructions.

II

After all, she looks out, a slight turn
and her cheek is against the blind, she sees
the boats are coming home, their path

curved and yielding to the current;
they scatter and cluster again, to follow
into the small harbor, one by one;

when the last one has passed under the tower
the light of evening is offered—
like a bowl that is offered, held in both hands,
the milk-white light fills
the whole wide empty bay.

Allow Plenty of Time

Can I pause, will there be time to pause
along the way, how long will it last,
that spell when I can't move and can't turn a page,

before facing the road? The Russians in *War and Peace*
before the failed abduction, the smokers
outside the slow café, watching

a slow goods train stretching itself out—
they all do it naturally and don't need
a tap on the glass or a church bell

to make them shiver and then
slowly begin again.

The Cat Dinner

We knew they were there, their flattened black masks,
and that when they withdrew into lunar shadow
there would be no witness, a cobwebby silence.

Lips open but speech fails, round the half-cleared table,
sitting there, but strangers, our fussy notes shuffled,
lying at random. We made the long journey

to deliver the gesture, but who has noticed us?
Like the food left outside for visiting spirits
which is gone next morning, but did the cats eat it?

A Map of Convents

for Margaret MacCurtain

Cove Lane

"…and I took in children by degrees, not to make
any noise about it in the beginning. In about
nine months I had about two hundred children."
—Nano Nagle

Here is the map, with the underground streams,
the vessels that shrug at their tether, the walled islands,
and the fine gardens. There was another map,
of a different place, in her head; she told nobody.

Nothing gave her away, not her clothes,
or the clothes of her company, secular and plain,
or the cabin in the southwest corner
where now the playing field is hard ground.

It was poor like the shacks and cellars
piled together in the laneways
that sloped up from the South Channel.
The map of the city never showed
those children swiftly assembling
into a parliament of girls and boys.

Work

Try it again, says the voice. After that
a tinkling, the last piano lesson
joins up with the mutter of Latin,
the scholarship class getting a final trot
through the metrics of Horace's *Odes*—
and soon it will be all stillness indoors.

Now silence is waiting, a music from under the floor
too deep to be heard, a procession pacing
with tall faded banners that sway and swallow
the laneways' clatter and the brewery smell.
It flows like a tide, it encloses our evening.
It's as if we grew gills like fish to breathe it in deeply.

Inside the House

She crossed the footbridge, the bell
was ringing from the chapel, they were there
expecting her. In she went,
inside, like breathing, her quest
for the kernel, the seed
that might burst and make a way
of release for her, escape—
even if its hiding place was a shell,
even if it had to be hidden
like the fragile yolk that held the giant's life:

she plumbed the basement and searched inside the chimneys.

She laughed telling the story.
Oh, you'd do that, she said,
we couldn't have a man inside the door.
The kitchen chimney,
and I loved it,
well I remember
the old days, you'd be
black all over after it.

Chapel, 2014

When the rubble is piled in the chancel,
when the eye goes astray
in confusion and the light
entering by the usual window
pauses, at a loss, failing,
missing the usual gleam,
even their shadow scatters
here were they were gathered
in their full bodily presence,

but this is a house of levels
in a city of ridged hills—
the brothers asleep in the crypt
going on two centuries now,
the parlor down at street level
where the girls came for their lesson
still furnished. Empty upstairs the rooms
of those who were absent with permission,
where they studied, where they wept.

A Roomful of Seicento Frames

When the invaders rifled the convents
they brought these trophies away
and the curious may visit them, here
in the New Wing. Not only St. Catherine
in crimson and pale blue, St. Peter Martyr,
his head cloven, St. Agatha,
St. Margaret with her dragon, but then,
at the side, in the little room,
there is just a scant collection
of empty frames, polished, ornate—
the visitors glance in at them
and pass along, puzzled by the display,
these flourished shapes enclosing
only the wall hanging, dark damask.

I might move on to the long gallery
where the domestic scenery
displays itself at its best,
blond headed families grouped and mingling,
some out of doors, their tall trees shading them,
dandling their tailored sleeves—

but I stay for now, alone
with the frames, their gilded spirals
half shaped like the ring made
by fingers and thumbs of both hands,
their dark stained quotes, twisted,
curved like the martyr's ribs; like ivy
they shine, they clasp, but it's emptiness
embraced. The scenes (imagine
a triumph with captives, or a judgment
with pillars and guards all ready)—
the scenes are all missing, though the guarded ovals
bleed and reek, the sliced poplar
shifts like a hand mirror offering

a better view of what stank worse
than even the painters could tolerate
in the days when the authorities
advised them to be at their windows
to observe executions, to capture
the reality, to get it right.

The Small Museum

Enormous in the low crypt
(and even taller winged attendants
are offstage pressing to get inside)
the alien vested saints have
waited to manifest, they pounce
and lift up the despicable body,
they place it at the center, the point
where order meets disaster.

We need to be here, our signatures
(which not many will read) must populate
the lower margin, while
on an upper floor of the universe
the man, gigantic and bare, embraces light,
seeks brighter light, ignores the mob
as if he had met us in his own house,
naked at dawn, and we shrink seeing him
since the rising sun and shadows make him
tall as the judge on the day of anger.

Sister Marina

"Was there no drama in their lives?"
Once, it was almost Passiontide
and in Lent of course no letters arrived—
people knew better than to write.
So, when a letter landed postmarked Lancaster
for Sister Marina, Reverend Mother
opened and read it and went to find her
just leaving an empty classroom. She closed the door
and handed over the letter. Reverend Mother
was by two years the younger;
now for the first time in her life she saw
a face dragged backwards, dragged down, and how
pain and fear come first, and only about
two seconds later the beginning of thought
weighing down on the heart. She saw the brother's wife,
the brother grim-faced as ever, the sick child
as they printed on the other woman's mind,
as plainly as if a light had flickered
and lit them up in a screened picture.
Nothing that happened after so clearly displayed
how the body is all summed up in a face,
in a flaw—how knowledge travels all the way
down through a body and burns into the floor.
That was drama, she thinks, and hopes for no more.

To the Mother House

The tender heaved on its way across,
the liner floated grand in the harbor, and the girls
afraid of looking back picked out a porthole
and stared and waited for this parting to be over.

There was a war coming, there was work. The novices
would never see a soldier, only smile
at meager faces in the alpine sanatorium.
They nursed the miners hammered in the pit,
learning their obstinate love, meeting the mistress
who came after a death with a cushion
to go in the coffin, embroidered with *Bébé*.
The older nun lived through Ravensbrück, sent there
after hiding a crashed airman in the laundry.

II

Sister Clara, Sister Antony, meeting a niece
in the quiet convent garden in Desvres,
are overheard reminiscing, always in French,
about their first convent on the hill in Cork
and its precious holdings, the Penal Chalice,
the letters from an Italian priest (it's hoped
soon to be beatified), the foundress's diaries,

and all that was sent from the mother house: wine and brandy,
lace, the little medals blessed and certified
in Rome, in the Holy Year. A relic of the True Cross
in its gold box, a fine linen alb embroidered
in Portugal by a novice. Marble for the shrine.

The marble is there still, under the altar.
The mule-driver's curses, the rattling ass and cart
leave no sign on the stone; it sucks in meaning.

Marble is perfect, how it shows the bones
inside the skin, the folds in the light shroud,
and the trailing strands of hair.

Work

The oldest of all the sisters has to string
little pink beads on the edges of *Agnus Deis.*
She has a basket of the silk badges
and she gets through the heap while she thinks
about prayers and her life. But can she be sure?
What did the sister say only just now,

I hadn't felt that way since... 1946...
and wasn't it later than that, the move
to this house from the old convent?
If she wasn't so stiff she would walk herself,
leaning on her stick up as far as the graveyard,
and check the dates on all of the early crosses.

Carr's Lane

You can see the tall front door
but don't expect to be admitted.
On your left is Carr's Lane,
at the corner a newspaper shop;

up the lane a doorway, steps
worn pale by rain and people climbing,
unlocked at the agreed time
on quiet days for callers they know.

Scholars disagree about
Carr's Lane, is it *cart's lane* corrupted?
Or was there a prosperous
local merchant family called Carr?

They could have grown rich selling
butter to the transatlantic trade
or beef abroad. If their books
gave their story those have all been cleared.

The dealer came one Monday
early, the shelves were bare before noon,
the library is closed off—
dangerous, woodworm in the floorboards.

For James Connolly

When I think of all the false beginnings...
The man was a pair of hands,
the woman another pair, to be had more cheaply,
the wind blew, the children were thirsty—

when he passed by the factory door he saw them,
they were moving and then waiting, as many
as the souls that crowded by Dante's boat

that never settled in the water—
what weight to ballast that ferry?
They are there now, as many

as the souls blown by the winds of their desire,
the airs of love, not one of them weighing
one ounce against the tornado

that lifts the lids off houses, that spies
where they crouch together inside
until the wind sucks them out.

It is only wind, but what braced muscle, what earthed foot
can stand against it, what voice so loud
as to be heard shouting *Enough?*

He had driven the horse in the rubbish cart, he knew
the strength in the neck under the swishing mane,
he knew how to tell her to turn, to back or stand.

He knew where the wind hailed from, he studied
its language, it blew in spite of him.
He got tired waiting for the wind to change,

as we are exhausted waiting for that change,
for the voices to shout *Enough*, for the hands
that can swing the big lever and send the engine rolling

away to the place I saw through the gap in the bone
where there was a painted house, fiddling and the young people
dancing on the shore, and the Old Man of the Sea

had been sunk in the wide calm sea.

III

The sea moves under the wind and shows nothing—
not where to begin. But look for the moment
just before the wave of change crashes and

goes into reverse. Remember the daft beginnings
of a fatal century and their sad endings, but let's not
hold back our hand from the lever. Remember James Connolly,

who put his hand to the work, who saw suddenly
how his life would end, and was content because
men and women would succeed him, and his testament

was there, he trusted them. It was not a bargain:
in 1916 the printer locked the forme,
he set it in print, the scribes can't alter an iota—

then the reader comes, and it flowers again, like a painted room.

The Bookshelves

These are our cliffs, where we hang and grope and slide.
Why should there be a path upwards among such casual
stacks? Somebody shelved them size by size
but still they signal throbbing on shadow types.
Their lightning blazes like a faraway headlight
bound firmly elsewhere. Most times
it's the finger tucked in the big dictionary that leads
onward (as if under submerged voussoirs, along
damp paving to the ancient reservoir) to tell us
that the jumping flashes on the rockface were the codes
for a name that we could never have otherwise known.

Maria Edgeworth in 1847

*"She was touched by the generosity of the porters who carried the rice and India
meal to the vessels for shipment to Ireland in the famine, refusing all payment;
and she knit with her own hands a woollen comforter for each porter, of bright
and pretty colours, which she sent to a friend to present to the men, who were
proud and grateful for the gifts; but, alas! before they received them, those
kind hands were cold, and that warm heart had ceased to beat."*
—Frances Edgeworth, *A Memoir of Maria Edgeworth*

Anger. *Work*. Confusion—what is to be done?—
the Atlantic in the way and the news getting worse,
work stretching to occupy every hour in the day,
carrying back and forth, lifting, bearing and setting down.

We are in the centuries when work told the body how
to lift, fasten and drag, the weight of the world needed heaving,
when the horses staggered and slowed on the steep hill,
the coach too full, too heavy to drag onwards—

they stopped fearfully and the child from the cabin
was waiting for his chance, he ran out with a stone,
pushed it behind the wheel so the horses could breathe
and waited for the farthings flung from the passengers' windows.

Now he is carrying sacks of meal to the boat,
back and forth, loaded then free, and the work stretching ahead
like the road where at the same moment Maria Edgeworth
walks out, her young servant beside her carrying

the basket that gets a bit lighter
at every cabin door. This is her work now
at the end of her life. At home,
she sits down to the story she is writing,

line after line, her hand straying back and forth
across her remaining pages. The child from the cabin
is a man carrying meal to the docks, and at last
the day is over, and time for him to be paid—

but he is too angry, his colleagues are too angry
to take money for helping to feed starving people. And she
who is not ever recorded as being angry
takes out her knitting needles and the long skeins of wool

the women have spun in the cabins, to make
a warm comforter for every man, her needles
twitching back and forth until the work is done.
She is famous and fortunate, she will be remembered.

Like the girl whose brothers were turned into swans,
she does what she knows, the long scarves piling
softly beside her chair, one after the other like the days.

The men are far from home when her gift reaches them, the trace
of their work unraveling like a worn thread of wool, their kindness
out of anger stretched out across the Atlantic, for an answer.

The Faces

I WOMAN IN A TRAFFIC JAM

I still see the woman, a drowned
face rising up out of a wave,
time combing back strands of her hair.

I see her now just as clearly
as when we traveled beside her;
the man was raging at the wheel

as in forty minutes we moved
and paused again in jammed traffic;
she had her knitting out, her face

never altered. A mile ahead
some disaster made a headline;
sometimes we inched forward, sometimes

they slid ahead by a few yards.
It was like history, held there
in view of another lifetime:

we climbed the cogged wheel of our age,
our century, side by slow side.

II THE COBBLER OF SPILIMBERGO

So through a thickened lens of time
I see clear over centuries
Domenico the cobbler,
his face a metaphor, like her

actual face, held still. He owned
these three books: *The Decameron,*
Orlando Furioso and

a vernacular *Testament,*
and when the inquisitors came
and confiscated all of them

he swore *I'll never read again.*
I see his eyes, they are searching
for words vanished, the wave of time

sweeping over him with headlines
he cannot read, gripped in traffic,
his fate redacted, his eyes blank.

The Capture

First, I need help to make the frame, with wings
and a nose and a tail fin,
room for those thick-furred beasts
if they scramble up or settle out of the air,
and a crack to harbor seeds for a trail of leaves,

so when I leap away the horizon swings
in the far distance, the hills
are floating like smoke, the fields
and the valley exposed, then diving, the plane
flashing, and in every hollow under the leaves

a life huddles listening for a note that stings
music into life, a song that jumps, that grieves.

Except that I am not the earth but a late map of this earth,
its hedges tacking me down, don't expect me
to race again. The yearly bands of children
at school under the hedges are memorizing
their alphabets and fluxions and the distances
grow longer with every name called on the roll.

I could eclipse and cloud them with a wink
as there's no room left in the passages of my brain
for every conversation between the slug and the leaf,

yet if I follow the slow air where it spreads tracking
the laboring boats across the oceans,
where it knocks at every door and pushes inside,
where it winds along roads in France beside
the daughters leaving home to serve strangers,

the sons in foreign fields, the one holding
King Louis' hand on the scaffold as he prays,
the earth recedes.

Can they all be crammed and keyed, "the Irish race
through history," which terms do we lack, to hold
that frame together, and how can we see anything
without the frame?
                    If I am a screen flickering
between the four handpainted provinces
and the bricks and timber,
this roof that shelters me,

I should find the bits of the frame,
I should walk around them to see if
they could be matched awry, to a different plan,
then try if I can persuade them
to limp back over the hedges, and
if then I'll feel the weight of the beasts
as they settle again along the mismatched wings.

Monsters

Now that there's nothing I don't understand,
why do they come to me with their informations?
They come in my dreams with their highlighting pens,
they tell me the roman numerals
on the shelf-end panels in the cathedral library
have all been regilded, someone has worked
with agate and crows' feathers to raise
gold flourishes and leaf script capitals. Show us,
they ask, the book that opens like a curtain;
and I tell them about the day I met
Ovid in the street, and he passed me
without a greeting.
                    He had just thought
of the words that made the shrouds and tackling
swell with small buds, then looping stems,
then five-pointed leaves of ivy
catching, clutching the oars.

When I read it again myself I can see the oarsmen
frozen at their work, the sleepy drunk youngster
they were planning to sell, who wept
when they tied his hands, all of a sudden in charge,
his forehead ornate with grapes—
he is balanced on delicate sandals,
watching how they change, their spines
curve, they dance in the waves, each man
a monster to his neighbor.

Space

She has looked for a space, empty so she can grow,
and three dimensions seemed enough. The room
contains her, the white ceramic tiles visible
beyond the archway, where the low door thrown open
swings: all is void, and the packed stuff
menacing her for months in toppling stacks
is cleared and abandoned

                              —just

then without warning
down on the river
the ship that lay moored
for three whole days, its
temporary lights,
empty decks shining,
begins its journey
again, silently,
stiffly almost, down
to where the river
spreads wide and smooth
open to the tides
and slips off—smaller—
out on the channel.

View

Now the traffic pauses, *now,*
help me to climb on the table,
then a leg up to the window sill,
and then I'll turn, my right knee
cold against the copper pipes,
to get a view. If anyone looks
they can see the tear in my stocking,
but the view—

       right into the room
through to the alcove where the portrait
used to hang. Such a long time,
and when the wind stops blowing
the curtain across I can see
the shape on the wall. It's a line of dust
against the pale blue-green.

At least that's real; the portrait is gone.
It was a woman, the eyes
clearly reflecting a shrunken image,
St. Sebastian, seized,
bound, for a martyr. Once he occupied
the whole wall, the tall space
behind the high altar—

       now
when I look into her eyes I see him,
the ruined pillar, the antique stones,
his elegant writhing body and
her eager eyes making him shrink
as the dusty line
calls me to view her, *now,* on the shadowed
pale blue-green wall.

The Light

for Damhnait Ní Ríordáin

Come out, I say, and you all come to the light.
I look for her, she's there,
the sunlight glancing up from the shining leaves
wavers on her face
as she consults the rose bush, the light moving
in slow time with her hair.

At the end of the garden where the tall trees shivered
the river was in spate.
We walked down there at dawn to get rid of the noise
of the night's debate,
leaving the table with the bottles and empty glasses,
Socrates and his fate

in *Phaedo,* in the Great Books of the World edition
on thin Bible paper
laid open, we left them to look at the river rushing
down to Askeaton,
the tall Desmond castle, the friary beyond the bridge,
in their desolation.

When we turned back, to wash the glasses and arrange
the room before her parents
rose up, she stopped to consult the rose bush, the risen sun
blazed in its ranges;
her face shone green in the glancing light, I remember
across all the changes—

and that they had arrived in the dark, the small shy moths
lined up, wings packed tight,
crowded under the lamp that still shone emptily
recalling the hours of night.

The Raging Foam

for Leland Bardwell (February 1922–June 2016)

I

Everything is late after an awful spring,
the morning sun, floating among clouds
when it ought to be shining between those two tall trees,
the fresh blue flower that should be here
to catch the light, making the minute real,
not open yet: they miss their yearly meeting.
I hear the news of her death and I wonder,
the seat behind her house that was a suntrap,
right by the sea, the waves
splashing and foaming on the rocks below,
is the sun late there, is there only shade?

II

The foam breaks and withdraws.
It's a scatter of moments remembered,
my life, her life; and I gather them all up,
old scenes that are broken rumors
thrown high by the waves
(the horses swimming to the pier,
the baby in her cradle tossed
into the waiting currach). A segment
I recognize, the foam,
soapy water under a boat's side;

and looking down now in the profound
bay of memory, trying to guess how deep,
I see her in a ladylike tweed coat placing
black spectacles to read in a clear
ladylike voice, the night Patrick Kavanagh died:
Walk on serenely, do not mind
That Promised Land you thought to find…

III

I know the date Kavanagh died, I know the date
in two-thousand-and-thirteen we lost her
on the train to Cork and found her again on the station
walking on serenely accompanied
by the remote jingling of the keys
of all her houses, the voices of all the strays
remembering the floors they slept on,
the unhooking in the small hours.

IV

And even in the late nights
when the house was full already,
they dragged it out, the *Raging Foam*
for the last of the latchicoes with no home to go to.

V

The wild girl in Leixlip, the mother in London,
her children dancing half-naked in summer
on Karl Marx's grave, the woman I rode out with
in the Phoenix Park on the little polo ponies,
which was later than some places and before so many others—
I remember, or she told me, or someone had the story,
but as the sea rises up to flood the pools between rocks
making one shining surface of rising water
where all the reflected lights floating shine together,
they carry the glint of all the colors,
the headstalls of horses, the written pages and her face:
they are there with scraps and overnight guests and children
claiming, allowing no precedence, only the black cat
crouches on its dry shelf of time, the last of a dynasty of kittens.

Seaweed

for my grandparents,
Thomas Dillon and Geraldine Plunkett,
married 23 April 1916

Everything in the room got in her way,
the table mirror catching the smoke
and the edges of the smashed windowpanes.
Her angle downward on the scene
gave her a view of hats and scattered stones.
She saw her brother come out to help
with the barricades, the wrecked tram
blocking off Earl Street, then back inside.

And for the man in the room, obscured
by her shadow against the window,
the darkening was a storm shifting his life—
he wondered, where were they now, and would
this perch above the scene blow apart soon,
and he imagined the weeds that sink their filaments
between rocks to nourish a life in water
until all of a sudden they're sheared away to sea.

And out at sea the gunboat was bucking and plunging,
throwing up spray. The weeds are slapped
back again on sharp rocks beside beaches
that are sucked bare by the storm after this one,
their holdfast plucked away. He was thinking,
would they find a place and lose it, blown away
again, and find another, on the western coast,
as the seaweed is landed, a darkness in the dark water.

A Slow March

Lento, as a threshold wearing down,
as the hesitant writer's hand,
the man with the trombone
stands waiting for the moment,
for the horn solo to finish, for the pause
until he lifts the long slider.

No other tone brings the body
so close, and how does it speak
about distance too? declaring the presence
of a breathing body, the note steady
as the lungs are slowly pushing out air
and the sound travels for miles,

while the girl with the piccolo is still
waiting her turn, for her five bars,
watching while he plays, her stance
as stiff as the pins holding her hair
flattened in place, gripping it down—
one eye on the score, counting the repeats.

And what harm if these characters
were to wear down to a trace and be lost
like the bump of an old defensive wall?
It would still take longer than
the notes of the trombone
and the piccolo too, fading away.

Fastnet

The winds go past, and the waves,
they forget where they were aiming
like a mind whose door is blown open
by another life imagined,
If only, forgetting the present:
Oh, any time, not now, anywhere
but not here, and the storm
sticks to us, a tall shadow marching
beside us, big as a darkening cloud—

no way of slowing down,
another life compelling,
and the wind is a Gothic parade
with faces like Castlereagh
seven bloodhounds beside him
panting for wider carnage,
faces that zoom and then pull back
and each of the serial lives is
plunged and then dragged to the surface.

Only the man that minds the light,
watching the great revolving spokes
hitting the piled castles of spray,
can say, trapped, not able to save,
This is life, I am living it now,
here, and the rock answers him back
as they wait for the storm to change its key,
It is yours, yours alone, you are living it here.

An Informant

When I asked her about the fate of the mission ship
sent away so many years ago
(and we knew then they'd be lucky to make land)
I could see she knew. She couldn't stop talking,
but her words sounded foreign.
I heard her sigh at last, taking off her gloves,
then silently picking up one of the lamps,
and she moved to the front door.
It was stiff, it hadn't been opened
since the last visit of the Vicar Forane,
but we found the key and pulled it wide.
She laid the lamp down in the doorway
and looked along the broad walk, to the gate
that is a roofed arch, with an alcove
intended for laying down a coffin,
so the bearers could take a rest. Sighing,
lifting the lamp, she carried it down there,
and I understood the words she used,
and what she wanted, for the action
to be complete. That we would leave it
there in the archway until the oil was spent
and the lamp died of its own accord.

The flame that had flickered pale in the daylight
shone steadily in the deep shade of the arch.
This is the short form, she said, we must
do this at least. This much we owe their names.

Hofstetter's Serenade

(Máire Ní Chuilleanáin, 1944–1990)

I felt the draught just now as I was keying in the numbers—
the date of her death, going on twenty-five years ago;
it is May but the bright evening is turning colder,
the tight bundle of grief has opened out and spread
wide across these years she knows nothing of, and if I go
in search of her I must unwind and stretch out the thread
she left us, so it twines like a long devious border
turning between the music stands, over and under
the kettledrums and the big bass lying on its side;
but it plunges away leaving the concert hall behind
and catches her at the start, in the year she was eleven, when
it first rose out of her, the pure line of sound that grows
rising dipping never landing twice on the same spot, then
catching its breath and then flowing along as even
as her own breathing, smooth like a weaver's thread
back and forth tracing. It weaves and it hops again,
the arched finger nails down the note but it overflows.

She was eleven years old. A thousand years before,
she could have been married to an emperor, she was sure
she was able to consent on the spot, as the notes wrapped around her, and
she went on playing as her eyes opened. Like words,
like the long serpent that can only swim upstream, like time,
the line drew her along, the string and the bow, towards
the moment I saw the breath leaving her body, and the silence began.

The Morandi Bridge

Let me lean my cheek against this limestone pillar—
I want to press until I feel the buzzing,
the sound the world makes when it isn't going
anywhere, a purr of grey transparent wings

hovering in one place. A humming to itself
because it needs to lie still, stay quiet and
recover, and who will bring help?
                              The noise
when the bridge fell down in Genova—the road

you and I drove along slowly, heading east
behind a small Fiat, packed and weighed down
with people, cake and flowers for a mother-in-law
who made a Sunday lunch; they were taking their time—

it was lunchtime again each year when we reached the bridge,
and the families were always on the move,
so we'd drive along slowly, those fifteen minutes
high up over the factories and streets—

I would tell you this news if the stones of the world
could carry language, but after eight months, the shock
and the noise inside them still, they cannot move
or even allow a message to pass through.

April 2019

New Poems

Nessus

He feels the new shirt closing against his skin,
close as damp leaves on the cooled earth,
but closer then, as a wave that assaults that
soaks everywhere, blinding,
grabbing like a body that can't get enough,
and I watch the sleeve beginning to burn,
though no flames yet. Soon there will be smoke
wrapping him round, covering over his name—

that woven stuff, I remember
I was lost in it years ago,
now I am back there, beside him as the flame
wears him thin. The seams I had worn out:
I see them mended whole again,
remade, and tailored to his measure.

Her Work

for Janet Mullarney

Just shadows, like all that we create,
one of them flaunts a core of bright red,
exposed; it is the lining of a mouth

surprised, gasping, shaking—then who knows
what others might hide, those deft shadows
that dive and pounce for a place to land?

At first she can only guess their form
as distance shrinks and multiplies them,
right until the last place they finish;

but she catches them, her grip shaping
measuring pressing the fertile twist:
a new life, captured against the light.

As a child makes dolls obey her call
the stuff she holds shudders yields and warps
into a word, and now in focus

no longer looks like a talking bird—
handled and human, the color scuffed,
a female head, eloquent, angry.

She'll never wash all that stain away:
the colors have spread under her nails,
her hands dipped deeper, wet with shadows.

The Line

Keep on watching the line, the way it dives
and swims, oblique, persistent,
back up to the level, that curve
and push, as the otter speeding in the stream:

the shape of desire, *sinuous,* from *sinus,*
a recess in the shore, a mapped bay
curving to a headland out of the long
sweep of a beach, white sand resting a season—

and the yellow leaves too gather and are blown
in just that curve, to cling along the edge
skirting the rocky woodland, a yellow line
that wavers, tapers and swells. But look closer:

all those lost coins of summer
do not amount to a line—
they only reveal where the line lies,
they only betray the place it hides.

A Scallop Shell

I looked for a purpose and I found one, walking
as far as the corner, and the next
corner after that, and then the next.

Suppose then that eventually I came
on a group sitting under a tree
that might almost serve as an image

(in wild faith, in impatience,
in kindness, in obstinate suffering),
an image of the human, whatever that is like—

and now they move a little, they seem
almost about to speak, but instead
one shrugs a shoulder, another

casts his eyes up to the branches shading them.
When one of them comes out with a word
acknowledging me, it's a complaint,

and then the big one says to the girl who spoke
"you're saying that just because…"
but another interrupts. She has stood up,

ignoring them, kicked over her chair
and the table, and walked away
across the road, where the traffic swiftly hides her.

Intimations

The first harsh cough out of the pipes
and then a violin tuning over and over,
those twisting harmonies: they are clearing the way.
The switching of the bow down close to the screw,
each vacillating scratching note,
probes into the old sore spot, patiently revisiting.
No music until that painful overture.

Not yet not yet is what they are saying
with the shiver among the strings, the bassoon
vibrating and a tread everywhere marching,
getting closer now. Light on the singer:
she stands ignoring a loose curl of hair
blown across her neck, her breath comes quiet,
shallow inside that extravagant bodice.

Not yet not yet, the deep inhalation
and the opening high note. How long to wait
for the liberating glance—*How long do I have,
do I seem trapped on the edge, will I ever
step away?* But this is the moment she loves
even if it wears patience to listen
to the flutes quavering. We want blood and arias,

and the big scene in the graveyard
where she rises from the tomb and sings
loud enough, long enough to send them all
scuttling home to silence.

The Relic

The last of our conversations ended suddenly. He said, "I will not see you again." A quick fidget, and he unshackled his left hand in its shining glove. The hand itself. He passed it over to me. It quivered, but I stashed it quickly in the depths of my satchel. I couldn't look at it for a week; when I put it in my desk drawer it wriggled and then settled, like a cat.

I couldn't make out how he'd manage without it. But when you told me he had died I asked, "and was he able to work?" "He had two hands in his coffin," you said. "He was holding a missal."

I looked for the hand again, to give it to you. When I opened the drawer, I jumped as a thumb detached itself as soon as I touched it. So that I would be able to keep that gift, or some of it at least.

The Blood Map

The map in my head is colored with the places
they took your blood, or we sat in a grey passage
waiting for an X-ray. In Ostia
they wouldn't keep you in the emergency ward,
they needed the trolley. In Madonna Alta
they sucked three dark red tubes out of your arm;
in Castiglion Fosco they rewrote the prescription
so you would have less to pay. In Terontola
we took an hour's break and went for lunch
in a cool bar, then back for the scans.

                           They said
you ought to have a second hip replacement—
which turned out not to be needed in the end.

Sasha, Died 10 March 2020

This cat was a heat seeker,
he would find a fireplace or a shoulder,
pushing his way, stretching a paw to restrain,
resting his chin on a protecting wrist.

Nothing showed more plainly how
we share that book of rules, buried
deep in the spine; when I was looking
for a space in the parking basement,

there it was, the stuttering signal,
getting warmer as I climbed,
three floors by the slow lift two corridors back,
leading me on past the shiny floors

and the dinner smell and the nurses' station
to the door of the room, where I paused,
until they had finished straightening out
the blue honeycomb blanket.

The Printer

The street: shadowy uprights
on either side, stalls
dismantled, overcoats busily
walking—not a crowd.
The streetnames shaded. Ahead,
light on the square, a bird
fluttering down to preen
perched on a chairback, and drink.

That overcoat is a man, head down,
closer now. The streetsigns blanked.
Only the old markethouse
I remember so well—where is the thread
I could follow—if only I could
make it back to that day in Venice,
I was angry like a fool
with you and the child, because
no school-work had got done.
I slammed outside and I walked
the tangle of passages,
I walked like someone searching,
hunting the language of childhood
and I fetched up then staring
at a tall house, in a square
the size of an apron; a stone notice declared
this was the printing shop where
Aldus Manutius practiced his trade.

Key-ring

The two little chrome discs between my fingers,
happily sliding past each other, both
belong on the same key-ring, which was yours—

one broader than the other, made to match
a common coin to be slipped in a shopping trolley —
on each of them is written Breast Aware.

The words are a dull pink, the letters cursive,
and the metal shines all the brighter, gleaming
to please me, warm now from handling.

I want to keep them near me forever.

Coda

Ag Stánadh Amach

Agus í ag stánadh amach, ina seasamh san áit sin, ag stánadh ag féachaint amach trí fhuinneog ard thuas staighre. An staighre ard deas caol, agus cairpéad uaithne air. Agus cad a chonaic sí ach slua mór daoine, ach nárbh fhéidir léi iad a fheiscint go cruinn soiléir mar gheall ar an sneachta a bhí ag titim le fada.

Cén fáth gur tháinig na focail sin ar ais chuici, focail na mná feasa?

Fear agus ualach mór á iompar aige go tuathalach, bean á leanúint, páiste ar a droim agus páiste eile ina láimh aici, cailín óg ag rith lena cois. Seandaoine ag luí siar fágtha ar deireadh. Agus an sneachta ag titim anuas gan stad, ag súrac gach imire óna mbalcaisí, iad ag cosaint a gceann is a n-aghaidh ar an ngaoth chomh maith agus ab fhéidir leo, ionas nach n-aithneofaí iad.

Aon bhábóg amháin ina láimh ag cailín beag, gúna bán uirthi agus ribín dearg. Cén fáth gur thugadar ribín dearg di, an tuar fola é sin?

Na daoine ag triall thart gan cabhair a fháil ó éinne, agus an oíche ag luathú. Iad beagnach dofheicthe ach bhí a fhios aici go rabhadar ann fós agus slua eile á leanúint. D'fhan sí ag an bhfuinneog go dtí gur éirigh an ghealach agus chonaic sí an taobh tíre: folamh, bán, sleamhain snasta. Bhí an ghaoth ina tost agus mar sin chuala sí na saighdiúirí i bhfad sar a thángadar i láthair. Fuaim na leoraithe i bhfad, ag brostú ar an áit, ag brostú i dtreo di.

Ach níor leagadar láimh uirthi, bhí sí socair sábháilte thuas staighre. Fiú níor tharraing sí an cuirtín, níor mhúch an solas. D'fhan sí ann agus a gúna corcra agus an cairpéad uaithne ag lonrú amach. Nuair a d'imigh siad d'fhágadar a rian ar an sneachta, agus ansan do thosnaigh an sneachta arís agus chlúdaigh an lorg.

Cén fáth gur tháinig focail na mná sin ar ais chuici? *At chíu forderg, at chíu rúad.* Nuair a tháinig Fedelm chun eolas a thabhairt don bhanríon faoi na rudaí a bhí le teacht, labhair sí as a carbad, is d'éist an bhanríon ina carbad féin. Ar an leibhéal céanna. Iad gléasta mar an gcéanna, éadaí ildathacha orthu araon. Ach mise, dúirt sí ina haigne féin, anseo mar atáim, socair sábháilte thuas staighre, ní fheicim ach an méid atá os mo chomhair, san aimsir láithreach. Nach leor san d'aon duine amháin?

Loinnir frithchaite ón sneachta á soilsiú.

Gazing Out

As she gazed out, standing upright in that place, gazing looking out of a high upstairs window. Fine high narrow stairs, a green carpet. Then what did she see only a great host of people, only that she could not see them clearly because of the snow that had been falling for ages.

Why did the words come back to her, the words of the wise woman?

A man awkwardly carrying a big bundle, a woman following him, a child on her back and another held by the hand, a young girl running at her side. Old people at the back, left behind. The snow ceaselessly falling, leaching every tinge from their old clothes, they shielded their heads and their faces as well as they could against the wind, in the hope of not being recognized.

A little girl holding a single doll, a white dress on her, a red ribbon. Why did they give her a red ribbon, does that stand for blood?

The people passing along without help from anyone, night coming on. Almost invisible but she knew they were still there and another host following them. She stayed at the window until the moon rose and she saw the countryside empty, white, smooth, clean. The wind had fallen silent and so she heard the soldiers long before they came. Noise of lorries far away, hurrying to the place, hurrying towards her.

But they did not lay a hand on her, she was safe and sound upstairs. She did not draw the curtain or put out the light. She stayed there, her purple dress and the green carpet shining out. When they were gone they left their track on the snow, and then it started to snow again and covered the traces.

Why did that woman's words come back to her? *I see them crimson, I see them red.* When Fedelm came to tell the queen what she foresaw, she spoke from her chariot, and the queen listened from her own chariot. On the same level. They were dressed similarly. Both dressed in many colors. But, said she to herself in her own mind, from this place I'm in, safe and sound upstairs, I can only see what is in front of me, in the present. Is that not enough for a single person?

The reflected light from the snow shining on her.

An Crann

An teach a d'fhágamar i naoi déag dathad is a naoi—
agus gan fhios ag éinne fós cé mhéad páiste
atá tar éis fás suas ins an áit chéanna ó shin—
maireann an crann a chuir m'athair ann,
ach cad a tharla don gcasán suiminte a leag seisean,
rud a theaspáin dom conas a thriomaíonn an tsoimint fén ngaoth?
Is ann a d'fhoghlamas conas mar a bhíonn an saol
idir mhnáibh is fearaibh, mo mháthair sa bhaile linne,
m'athair ag teacht abhaile, ise ag fiafraí as Gaeilge.
"'Bhfuil aon scéal agat?"
An cailín aimsire sa chistin, sneachta i mí na Nollag,

go dtí go bhfuaireas amach nach raibh an méad sin
ceart in aon chor. Chuamar go léir ar aghaidh
ar bhealach éigin eile, á leanúint
mar a fhásann an crann, gach géag ag nochtadh a léarscáil féin,
go dtí an lá go dtáinig an áit ar ais chugam
agus d'fhanas go dtiocfadh na focail, thosnaíos á dtóraíocht
ar leibhéal níos doimhne fós, díreach mar a chuardaíonn an phréamh
a bealach fé thalamh, ag lorg cothaithe is buntobair.

The Tree

The house we left in nineteen forty-nine—
and who knows now how many children
have grown up in that same place since then—
the tree is alive that my father planted there.
But what happened to the cement path he laid,
that showed me how cement dries under the wind?
That's where I learned how the world is
between men and women, my mother with us at home,
my father coming home, her asking him in Irish
"Have you any news?"
The maid in the kitchen, snow in December,

until I found out that all that information
wasn't true at all. We moved on
along a different road, that we followed
as the tree grows, every branch displaying a map of its own,
until the day the place came back to me
and I waited for the words to come, I began searching
in a still deeper seam, just as the root explores
its road underground, looking for sustenance and a source.

The Swan

Charles Baudelaire

I

Andromache, you are in my mind. That little stream,
the cracked looking glass that could never
capture the majestic scale of your grief,
a virtual Simois that swelled with your tears:

one drop from there seeded in my memory
as I passed through the new Place du Carrousel.
My old Paris has vanished (I'm shocked to find
the human heart more constant than a city);

the builders' huts are only memories now,
the half-carved columns, the gross lengths of pipe,
the weeds rooting between blocks of stone
stained green, puddles, rubbish in junk-shop windows,

among which used to be a wild-beast show.
There one morning, under the clear cold sky
when workers are awake, and the city cleaners
push their dark whirlwinds in the silent air,

I saw a swan escaped out of a cage,
his webbed feet bare on the dry paving-stones,
dragging white plumage on the filthy ground,
his beak wide open by an empty gutter,

he dipped his trembling wings in dust, demanding
(heart full of the smooth lake where he was born)
"Rain, when will you rain? When will the thunder sound?"
I see this wretched emblem, "the power of fate,"

raising his head against the sky, that pose
Ovid says is peculiar to man, jerking
his neck, his avid head at the cruel sky
as if his reproaches were for God in power.

II

Paris is changing, but in my melancholy nothing
has stirred. The new tall buildings, their scaffolds,
blocks, the tatty remains of old streets, all turn
allegorical. Precious memories weigh like stones.

I stand in front of the Louvre and the image strikes
again, my great swan madly gesturing,
ridiculous and sublime in that exilic fashion,
devoured by a desire beyond relief, and you

Andromache, fallen from the arms of your hero
Hector, a spoil for Pyrrhus to boast of, then
passed on to boring Helenus—no wonder
you crouch in ecstasy beside an empty tomb.

I think of the lean consumptive African woman
tramping through the mud, searching with her wild eyes
for absent palm trees, pride of her native place
hidden behind the massive screen of mist;

of all who have lost what never can be found,
never again—of those who feed on tears,
sucking on grief like a kind mother-wolf—
of slender orphans withering like flowers.

So in this forest where my mind's astray
an ancient Memory blows an insistent horn.
I think of sailors abandoned on an island,
prisoners, the defeated ... and so many more.

Kilcash

from the Irish, c. 1800, anonymous

What will we do now for timber
with the last of the woods laid low—
no word of Kilcash nor its household,
their bell is silenced now,
where the lady lived with such honor,
no woman so heaped with praise,
earls came across oceans to see her
and heard the sweet words of Mass.

It's the cause of my long affliction
to see your neat gates knocked down,
the long walks affording no shade now
and the avenue overgrown,
the fine house that kept out the weather,
its people depressed and tamed;
and their names with the faithful departed,
the Bishop and Lady Iveagh!

The geese and the ducks' commotion,
the eagle's shout, are no more,
the roar of the bees gone silent,
their wax and their honey store
deserted. Now at evening
the musical birds are stilled,
and the cuckoo is dumb in the treetops
that sang lullaby to the world.

Even the deer and the hunters
that follow the mountain way
look down upon us with pity,
the house that was famed in its day;
the smooth wide lawn is all broken,
no shelter from wind and rain;
the paddock has turned to a dairy
where the fine creatures grazed.

Mist hangs low on the branches
no sunlight can sweep aside,
darkness falls among daylight
and the streams are all run dry;
no hazel, no holly or berry,
bare naked rocks and cold;
the forest park is leafless
and all the game gone wild.

And now the worst of our troubles:
she has followed the prince of the Gaels—
he has borne off the gentle maiden,
summoned to France and to Spain.
Her company laments her
that she fed with silver and gold:
one who never preyed on the people
but was the poor souls' friend.

My prayer to Mary and Jesus
she may come safe home to us here
to dancing and rejoicing
to fiddling and bonfire
that our ancestors' house will rise up,
Kilcash built up anew
and from now to the end of the story
may it never again be laid low.

Hunger

after Langland, Piers Plowman, *Passus VI, 154–303*

When Piers the pilgrim went to the plough
in hope of the harvest of his half-acre
some workers came willingly to dig and ditch.

…but Waster reared up and would have words with him:
go and piss with your plough, you pennypinching preacher—
we'll not starve to please you, we'll steal if we have to,
your bread and your beef, and we'll live in spite of you.
I never worked, said Waster, and I won't start now,
and I don't give a fiddler's fart for the law
or for Piers or his party or his plough at all.
Devil mend you, said Piers, I'll do for you all now,
and he hallooed for Hunger who heard him at once:
show these louts for me they can't lounge for ever.

Hunger bound Waster about the belly,
he shrank his stomach until his eyes stared,
he battered the boasters about the cheeks
so they looked lanternjawed all their lives after,
he beat them down till their guts were bursting.
Then Piers with half a loaf called Halt! to Hunger.
Let them live, he said, and eat with the hogs,
or have beans and bran broken up together.

At wind of that word they were away to the haggard,
they threshed his corn till the night threatened,
so Hunger was squinting to have a sight of them,
all for a pot of pea soup Piers had made.
The clergy kilted up the skirts of their habits,
went out working with spades and shovels,
they dug, they ditched to drive away Hunger.
The blind and the bedridden were better by thousands,
the lame that lay idle were suddenly healed.
The dog's dish was dinner for many hungry
and the beggars were busy for a plate of beans,
the poor were pleased with peas for their wages
and eager to obey when Piers gave the order.

So Piers was proud and put them on his payroll,
gave wages for their work as he saw them worthy.
Then Piers had pity and bade Hunger go packing,
go back to his own place and stay there for good—
but whisper, he said first, how shall I handle them?
They'll do what I say as long as they're starving
and they are my brothers, bought with Christ's blood.
Truth once told me to treat them with love—
but if they won't work how am I to have my way?

Hear now, said Hunger, and hold it for wisdom:
big bold beggars that could work for their bread,
feed them hens' food and horses' food to help their courage.
Baffle them with beans when their bellies rumble
and if they complain call them to work.
As for the deserving cast down by disaster
or foundered by fraud, let them find your charity
for the love of Christ and the law of nature,
Alter alterius onera portate
let each one bear the burden of his brother.
The needy and the naked your goods should nourish;
if you wish for grace follow the Gospel:
Facite vobis amicos de mammona iniquitatis
let money and Mammon make you friends of the poor.

I would not grieve God, said Piers, for all the earth's goods.
May I do as you say without sin? he said then.
Yes surely, said Hunger, unless the Scripture lies.
Go to Genesis, the giant that engendered us all:
In sudore et labore shalt thou earn thy bread,
and *Sapientia* says the same, I saw it in the Bible,
Piger pro frigore would not till his field
and by that he shall beg and none abate his hunger;
and Matthew with the man's face mouths the same story,
the tale of the talents that must be traded
and the moral that was meant when the lord made judgement:
he that hath shall have, and help where it's needed,
and he that hath naught shall have naught and get no help
and even what he hopes to have shall be taken from him.

Well, said Piers, tell me something else,
do you have any little learning in leechcraft?
My company and myself have a curious complaint,
we're in bed all the week with an aching belly.
I know surely, says Hunger, what your sickness is,
too long at the table makes you groan and grouch.
Take no food until Hunger tells you,
arise before Appetite has eaten all his fill;
let this be your diet, I dare venture my ears
Doctor Physic may sell his furred hood for food.

By St. Paul, said Piers, I'll profit by your words.
Leave us now, Hunger, when you like, and *adieu.*

By God, said Hunger, I've no notion of going
until I have dined and drunk in your house.

I have no money, said Piers, to buy meat,
I have two fresh cheeses and some curds and cream,
two bran loaves baked with beans, no bacon,
parsley and carrots and scallions in my garden.
I've a cow and her calf and a cart mare
to draw dung to my field while the drought lasts;
that's all we have to live on till the day of Lughnasa,
and then I hope to bring home the harvest
when I can design your dinner with the dearest.

All the poor people fetched in pea pods,
beans and baked apples they brought in their laps,
chives and chervil and plenty of ripe cherries,
a present to Piers to pay off Hunger,
and Hunger ate in haste and howled for more—
the poor folk for fear fed Hunger fast,
with green roots and peas to poison him they planned—
but now harvest was near, new corn was come home,
they rejoiced and fed Hunger the finest of food
and good ale as Glutton hinted, and bade their guest sleep.

Song of the Woman of Beare

from the Old Irish (ninth century), anonymous

Low tide. As with the sea.
Age darkening my skin.
Even as I struggle
age grabs and likes its meal.

I am the nun of Beare.
The shirt I wore was fresh
always. Today I'm worn,
an old shirt sees me out.

The main chance, the money
draws your love not the man;
in our day flourishing
our joy was the human.

Human goodness pleased us,
delight on our journeys
wearing out days with them
and no boasting after.

Look at them now: they crow,
they claim, they do not yield,
they part with little, then
boast of how much they gave.

Carriages, prizewinning
fast racehorses, the gifts
of those high days: God bless
the giver's open hand.

And now my body craves
homing to where it's known;
let the Son of God choose
the time to claim me back.

These bony slender arms
of mine—the ones I once
owned, how they used to like
embracing those great kings.

As they look now, my arms
are slender and bony,
hardly worth the trouble
lifting to hug young boys.

Girls are glad to welcome
May as it draws near;
this season saddens me,
pitiful, an old one.

I don't join in sweet chat;
no bride-feast is prepared;
thinning and grey my hair
suits the cheap veil on it.

I don't object: a white
veil covering my head
rather than colors I
wore in my drinking days.

The old attract no envy—
but what about Feimen;
I wear out old clothing,
Feimen is clothed in flowers.

The Stone of Kings in Feimen,
Rónán's hall in Bregon:
long the storms are beating
weathered ancient faces.

The wave on the high sea
roaring, raised by winter,
forbids all visits now:
high and low keep away.

I know what they're doing,
rowing over and back;
the reeds of Áth Alma,
they sleep in a cold place.

The sea I sailed on, those
days, was youth—long ago.
Years took my looks from me,
cooled my first young ardor.

The time is long today,
even when the sun shines
I need my covering,
I am feeling my age.

Summer of youth I knew,
I wore out, then autumn,
winter that ages all,
I feel it beginning.

I wore out my youth first,
and glad I did. How would
my dress be newer now
if I had played safer?

It was a fine green dress
my king spread on Drumain;
the worker knew his craft,
coarse stuff turned to new wool.

And I am in sadness—
each acorn must decay—
I feasted with candles
but the chapel is dark.

My days drinking spirits
and wine with kings are gone.
Now it's a soft drink, whey,
water with the seniors.

I'll stick with the soft drinks,
God's will limiting me,
living God let me pray,
keep me far from anger.

My dress is marked by age,
my sense is gone astray,
my hair is grey, I'm like
an old tree's withered bark.

My right eye was taken
to buy eternal land
and now the left eye goes
to complete the payment.

The wave at high tide, then
the tide falling again—
what high tide fills for you
is emptied by low tide.

The wave at high tide, then
falling tide that follows:
I know them, I have seen
full tide and low water.

The wave at high tide—how
silent my storehouse now:
once I fed multitudes,
a hand fell on them all.

The Virgin's son—who knew
he would enter my house?
If I did no good deed,
no one had refusal.

Man among the creatures
is most to be pitied,
never foresees low tide
when the tide is fullest.

I have had my high tide,
I have held to my trust,
Jesus Mary's son has
saved me from low-tide grief.

Well for islands at sea,
their high tide follows low
water; I do not hope
my tide will turn and flow.

Hardly a harbor now
seems familiar to me;
all that the high tide saw
low water drags away.

INDEX OF TITLES

Indented entries in the Index of Titles and Index of First Lines indicate parts of poems and sequences.